Directing Your Heart Out

Directing Your Heart Out

Essays for Authenticity, Engagement, and Care in Theatre

TOM DUGDALE

methuen | drama

LONDON • NEW YORK • OXFORD • NEW DELHI • SYDNEY

METHUEN DRAMA
Bloomsbury Publishing Plc
50 Bedford Square, London, WC1B 3DP, UK
1385 Broadway, New York, NY 10018, USA
29 Earlsfort Terrace, Dublin 2, Ireland

BLOOMSBURY, METHUEN DRAMA and the Methuen Drama logo are
trademarks of Bloomsbury Publishing Plc

First published in Great Britain 2023

Cover design by Ben Anslow
Cover image: Background splash black on paper. (© aekkawin / Adobe Stock)

A catalogue record for this book is available from the British Library.

A catalog record for this book is available from the Library of Congress.

ISBN: HB: 978-1-3503-3907-1
PB: 978-1-3503-3906-4
ePDF: 978-1-3503-3909-5
eBook: 978-1-4081-3908-8

Typeset by Deanta Global Publishing Services, Chennai, India
Printed and bound in Great Britain

To find out more about our authors and books visit www.bloomsbury.com
and sign up for our newsletters.

For my parents

Contents

About the Author

Tom Dugdale is Assistant Professor in the Department of Theatre, Film, and Media Arts at The Ohio State University, where he teaches courses in directing, devising, and acting. He has directed over thirty productions.

This book is for anyone who is interested in theatre directing. But honestly, it is for students most of all—especially students who are brand new to directing. There are not enough books out there for you. Despite being written by experienced teachers and practitioners, with a wealth of knowledge to share, many books on directing are weighed down with inside references, details, and jargon that are challenging to wade through. This is not helpful. You deserve instead a book that excites and activates you, in language that is welcoming and accessible. You deserve to be inspired by the opportunity and potential of directing, not overwhelmed by its complexity. Along the way, a few inside references to plays, theatre history, and rehearsal terminology will be necessary. When these appear in the text for the first time, I will put them in **bold** and explain them further in the Glossary. But I do promise to keep the name dropping to a minimum.

For too long, directing has been miscast as an intellectual activity. You may study directing in an academic environment, but at its core, directing is not academic. Directing is instinctive. It is much more working with the hands and the heart than with the head. This book is a path to directorial creativity and confidence through an awakening of your own voice and vision—because directing, like any artistic act, collapses without your feelings in the mix. I hope to inspire you to direct passionately, with conviction, rather than to direct correctly or right. For the purposes of our journey, what you believe in most deeply will always be right, as long as it is shared with grace and care for those around you, including your audience. My simplest definition of directing is *caretaking*: the director is the one who looks after everyone and everything in the creative process to the best of her abilities, day in and day out, until the work is done. And so, in the end, this is mainly a book about caring.

To do their work, directors need something to direct. They need a play. Sometimes you will be given a play. Other times you will have the chance to choose a play, and this is the scenario we will consider here.

How then do you decide which play to direct? The answer is quite simple: it should move you. It should either make you cry or make you angry. If the play makes you angry, you should be angry in collaboration with it, in solidarity with it, and not angry in the sense of disliking the play itself. Never direct something to prove your dislike or distrust of it. Your time will always be better spent setting aside a play you do not care for and redirecting that energy toward finding another play, a play you love and believe in. Why waste your time on something you dislike?

Tears are a reliable gauge of your love and belief in a play because tears sneak up on you. Tears are an involuntary response. Any time you experience an involuntary response to a play or any piece of art, take note. Tears upon reading strongly suggest you will be able to sustain your passion for the material long enough to conceive, rehearse, and complete the production of the play—a process that may take months or even years. Our tears mark us. They identify and rat us out, making it impossible for us to hide what we feel. They twist and muddle our faces, leaving us soggy and snotty, and where you might be inclined to retreat from such antics at other times in your life, I encourage you to embrace them in your play reading. But never fake tears. When we fake tears, we squander one of the few legitimate indicators of authenticity we possess. Fake tears, and all schools of theatre promoting them, should be avoided like the plague.

Another question to ask when considering directing a play is, "Am I willing to take care of these people for as long as it takes?" By "these people" I mean the characters in the play. If you do not care enough about the play's characters to look after them generously and lovingly—rising in the middle of the night when they wake you, attending to them first thing in the morning— do not bother directing the play. It will be better to find other material and characters who more readily inspire your attention and supervision. You should be prepared to look after all the play's characters, not just your personal favorites or the leads. There are no leading characters in life. Breath and blood flow through all of us equally, no matter how many lines we have.

Where should you look for a play that makes you cry? You do not need to look anywhere special. The library will do, or a friend's bookshelf, or a teacher's collection. You might consider plays that are mentioned in the newspaper and in reviews, and of course, if you are able to see plays in production, that is helpful, too. What is important is not so much *where* you are looking as *how* you are looking, and even more to the point, how you are monitoring your reaction to your search. You are reading for material that provokes a visceral response, the kind of sensation you might experience when you are startled by a loud sound, awestruck by a gorgeous landscape, or touched by the generosity of a friend. Meditate upon what these autonomic, authentic responses feel like in your body. Gazing into the watercolor brilliance of a sunrise or sunset, marveling at your child's tiny hand grasping your finger—and marking what ripples through your organism as you behold these miracles—will make you a better reader of plays.

Theatre is the most human of the arts. Other arts deal with people, but only theatre consistently situates human beings at the center of the work, in a continuous shared-space relationship to another group of humans, the audience. It will serve your play reading and your directing to get as interested as you can in the beauty and wonder of people. Set the bar high, seeking out plays that contain these wonders, that make your heart skip a beat. Some of you may insist tears are elusive for you, that your feelings are too buried to be useful in this search. Without wanting to challenge your position on this—you know yourself best—I would gently encourage you to remain open to the possibility of being moved. It may be that you are in fact quite disposed to tears but that you have been conditioned, like many of us, to squelch them.

We live in a society relentlessly organized toward productivity, where cool composure and self-control are prized over more emotional responses, which are often discouraged and even judged harshly. Over time, we become programmed to bury and silence those parts of ourselves that may act up, speak out, unpredictably. Yet making art is first and foremost an act of creativity, not productivity, and creativity springs from spontaneity and surprise. Where other pursuits are understandably skeptical of the unknown, theatre requires it. You can feel safe in theatre exploring those parts of yourself that you do not yet understand. Theatre makes space for you to acknowledge your beliefs, desires, dreams, fantasies, loves, pains, fears, anxieties, and ecstasies.

Seek out plays that will create free, open, and safe spaces of expression for what you feel and need to say. By no means am I advocating disobedience or any brand of individual expression that would jeopardize the wellbeing of yourself or those around you. But use theatre as a personal experiment in not holding back. Interestingly, in acknowledging more of what you feel, you strengthen your capacity to empathize. When we open ourselves to ourselves, we open ourselves to others, and this is crucial, since caretaking lies at the heart of directing. The first step toward deep and conscientious caretaking as a director is selecting material that makes your heart sing. Directing something you do not care about is irresponsible. When we nurture our care, we invite others to care, too. It is a viral process. Care is contagious.

Recently I was working with a bright directing student who presented an impressive concept for a production. The concept was accompanied by dazzling visuals. In exquisite detail, the student outlined the scenic, lighting, costume, and casting choices he would make. He shared plans to engage the audience in dialogue both before and after the performance. He offered a marketing and publicity strategy that was sure to catch people's attention. It was a thoughtful and comprehensive approach—except for one little thing. It was devoid of feeling. Nowhere had the student expressed how he *felt* about the production he was imagining or the play it would be based on. To put it bluntly, I could not tell if the student cared, and this undercut his work.

To direct is to continuously open windows through which others may glimpse your own passion and excitement, and by glimpsing it, ignite similar passions within themselves. When we find a play that stirs us, we stand the best chance of being at our most creative and catalyzing the creativity of everyone around us— actors, designers, producers, stage managers, and our audience. When you find a play that makes you cry, hold it tightly in your arms, and never let it go.

Take a play you will direct. Let us imagine it is **The Seagull** by **Anton Chekhov**, a play I adore. Smile at the play. It may have traveled a long way before landing on your desk. Then, open the play and remove each of its pages. Pull them loose from the binding, taking care not to rip or damage them. After you have freed all the pages, go to the first page, and using scissors, cut out the play's very first line of dialogue. In *The Seagull*, that line is:

Medvedenko Why do you always wear
  mourning?

Set that trimmed-out line aside, and then cut out the next line:

Masha I dress in black to match my life. I am
  unhappy.

Set your second trimmed line atop the first. Then cut out the third line, and the fourth, and the fifth, and so on, setting each successive line atop the last. Continue this process until a while later, you have trimmed out every line of the play. Place the last line atop all the other lines, taking care not to knock over the pile you have made, which by now is quite tall and perhaps gently undulating. Though this tower of lines now looks very different from the bound volume with which you began, it is still the play, since you have carefully excised and preserved each line. You have not modified the text.

Now, the next maneuver is rather challenging. You may want to take a deep breath before attempting it because it might make you nervous, but I have faith in your ability to pull it off. Carefully slide one hand beneath the tower of lines and place your other hand on top. Slowly raise the tower off your desk, and while exerting sufficient downward pressure with your top hand to hold everything together, rotate the whole column 180 degrees. It is possible a line or two might flutter free, and if that happens, don't worry about it. We can pick them up later. It's also possible the whole tower might disintegrate in your hands. I don't want you to dwell on this possibility of failure, but I want you to know the possibility exists, as it always must with any creative exercise worth attempting.

Let's assume for now that the rotation goes off without a hitch. Gently set the tower down at the corner of your desk. Be sure to keep your top hand in place until you have shimmied your bottom hand out. The tip-top of the tower should now be the very first line of the play once again:

Medvedenko Why do you always wear
mourning?

All the other lines should be stacked beneath it in the order in which they appear in the play. Carefully take that first line off the top of the tower, set it in the middle of your desk, and gaze at it. In isolation like this, the line jumps out at you, proclaiming its presence. It's like there's a spotlight on the line, demanding you analyze and ponder it. But you should avoid this until you have considered something much more important: the moment before the line. It is here, in the time and space *before* a line, that a director's work begins and is most concentrated.

Initially, this can be a challenging concept to grasp. More than a century ago, the Russian actor and teacher, **Konstantin Stanislavski**, theorized that human behavior could be understood as a series of desires pursued through **action**. Stanislavski called the character's desires **objectives**. Identifying a character's objectives became a fundamental task for the actor and director, and it remains fundamental to this day. Since a play is composed almost entirely of dialogue, it is tempting to try to identify a character's objectives from the lines themselves. It is tempting to ask, "When a character says X, what is she trying to do?" Unfortunately, you will not find a character's objective—at least not the root of it—in the line itself. Human beings speak because a desire has already been established. It is not our speaking that makes us want, *it is our wanting that makes us speak.* We do not start speaking in the first place until we have a reason to speak. Then, having spoken, we do not continue speaking until we revisit our objective—even if just for a millisecond—and find our desire still sufficiently pressing enough to warrant speaking again. This means that the time and space before the line—and between the lines—are just as important as the line itself. Rather than directing the line, the director should direct the space and time *before the line*.

In the instant before the line, the director creates the conditions that establish or re-affirm the character's objective. To direct is to create a very particular environment in which only a particular line—and no other—can sprout and flourish. When we see a performance and feel that the actor's delivery of the lines was so "natural" or "believable," we are witnessing directing that has properly attended to the moment before each line. It is as though the director has installed a ramp, delivering the actor perfectly to the line. This image also helps bring into focus the division of labor between director and actor. Although there is some overlap, the director should primarily attend to the moment before the line, leaving the actor to deal with the line itself. As soon as the line has been spoken, the responsibility shifts back to the director again, and the cycle goes on.

To direct is to painstakingly justify the existence of each and every line of the play, to ensure that nothing is overlooked or thrown away. If it sounds like a lot of work, it is, but it will imbue every moment of your directing with purpose and authenticity. You may find that once you have clarified the moments around the first several lines, it becomes easier to activate the moments around the lines later in the scene. This happens because the conditions you established early on continue to support and enable the dialogue so that all the lines start to feel immersed in a warm broth of justification. This is a good feeling as a director, and although you should not become complacent and must remain on guard for the odd line or two that requires additional adjustment, you can nevertheless relax a bit and take a step back. You have cracked what I like to call *the situation of the scene*. You have attended to enough of the moments around the lines to give the scene a momentum going forward, a momentum that allows the actors to take greater possession of the lines.

Let's put this idea into practice. Look back at the first line of *The Seagull* on your desk:

Medvedenko Why do you always wear
   mourning?

What could happen, what could we build in the space before this line, to make it utterly necessary for Medvedenko to say this? There are several possibilities, and I will offer two for your consideration. You may find it helpful to reference Appendix 2, where this scene between Medvedenko and Masha is printed.

Although this is the first line of the scene and the entire play, perhaps we are not seeing the start of a conversation, as the scene is so often staged. Perhaps we are instead being dropped into a dialogue that is already underway. In this case, Masha would have said something to prompt Medvedenko's question. Maybe she said, "I'm so hot." Since mourning attire and the color black can be heavy and warm in summer, it would be entirely appropriate for Medvedenko to respond to Masha by asking about her choice of clothing. This is one very simple way of justifying Medvedenko's line, and this approach reminds us that characters are always alive and active before a scene—or play—begins.

Here is another way of justifying Medvedenko's line. Again, let's assume Medvedenko and Masha have already been in conversation before the play begins, but let's imagine there has been a tremendously awkward silence between them— the sort of silence that can descend upon any couple who are still getting to know each other. When the play begins and the lights come up, perhaps we are dropped right into the middle of that silence. When the silence becomes unbearable for Medvedenko (and probably for the audience, too), he finally breaks it with his question.

Both of these ideas can work, though I am more drawn to the second, since it immediately establishes a deeper sense of relationship and conflict between the two characters. Here is how I would put this idea into action onstage:

The lights come up. Masha and Medvedenko sit on a bench. He looks at her. She stares straight ahead, her eyes hidden behind sunglasses. He looks away, then looks back at her again. She continues looking straight ahead but blows air with audible force out of her nostrils. He looks away again. He looks down at his shoe. He notices a tiny scuff. He licks his thumb and reaches down to rub out the scuff. Masha looks over at him as he's doing this and rolls her eyes behind her sunglasses. Medvedenko finishes with his shoe and, pleased with his efforts, turns and smiles at Masha. She musters a faint smile as she turns away from him, looking now toward the house. She sighs again and swats at a mosquito. Medvedenko sits back and looks up at the clouds in the sky. He starts to whistle, which annoys Masha, so she pretends to shift her weight, but really she is sliding down the bench away from him. She swats at the mosquito again. Medvedenko looks at her, stops whistling, then looks away, gazing out toward the audience. Masha massages her temples, kneading out the remnants of the hangover that has been with her all day. Medvedenko looks over at her once again. He takes a peppermint from his pocket and unwraps it. The cellophane is stubborn and makes an annoying sound as he struggles with it. Finally victorious, he offers the mint to Masha, but she doesn't move, her hands frozen on her temples, her stare frozen on the house. Medvedenko shrugs, pops the peppermint in his mouth, and gazes back out toward the audience. A half-minute passes. He looks back at Masha for the seventh time. She still hasn't moved. He looks down at the ground. Ten more seconds pass. The mosquito continues buzzing around them. Suddenly Medvedenko looks up and blurts out, "Why do you always wear mourning?"

Everything I describe here, if followed in detail, would take at least a few minutes to play out. That may feel like a lot, but it would undoubtedly establish conditions that would motivate Medvedenko's line. This example demonstrates how much construction can be done in the time and space before a line. By the time Medvedenko asked his question, the audience would crave something to fill the awkward silence just as much as Medvedenko does. It is powerful when an audience feels a need as palpably as a character does.

The simple truth is this: a line can never justify itself on its own. It will always need help and support. Nor can actors justify a line through pacing, intonation, or the loveliness of their voices. Sometimes actors try different ways of saying a line in an attempt to motivate it, emphasizing one word then another, but this is a futile effort. Lines are motivated when actors pursue clear objectives in response to conditions already in force before the line. Moreover, directors and actors will not find sufficient information about the characters— nor will they adequately build up the world of the play—if all they consider are the lines in the play. Think about all the time today when you have not been speaking. Even though you were not saying anything, you were still fully alive in these moments, your life continued. When we narrow our attention to just the lines of the play, we exclude at least half of the landscape of the play and amputate critical details of the characters' lives. Schools of directing and acting that focus on the text alone often explain their approach as a respect for the written word. Yet nothing could be further from the truth, since this "respect" ends up gutting the play of all the life that lives around the words.

Admittedly, I am being facetious with the title of this essay. Obviously, a play contains a text that has been carefully shaped by a writer, and the writer's work deserves our respect. When a director first encounters a play, and certainly when she begins preparing to direct it, she should read the text with great attention, carefully observing every detail the writer has included. But then it is essential that the director set the text aside, pretend it does not exist, and meticulously reconstitute it, line by line. This act of self-trickery—of knowing there is a text but pretending there isn't—is what I mean when I say, "There is no text." The director repeats this refrain to inspire herself to direct each line as if it never existed before.

Sometimes directors hesitate to embrace this approach for fear of adding too much business to the play. They worry about getting in the way of the text. While directing the time and space around the lines will create additional action onstage, as my example with Masha and Medvedenko illustrates, the new action will strengthen and deepen the validity of the text. It will be a catalyzing, beneficial act of construction, a bridge rather than a wall. In the most basic sense, we directors intervene to make a line work on the stage. With the understanding that we must always respect and serve the story set down by the playwright, we should never be afraid to build material around the lines, if we firmly believe our efforts enhance access to the lines—for actors and audience. The lines in a play are only the most visible and prominent features of an entire architecture that may extend deep beneath and between the lines. We cannot understand the towers poking up through the sand unless we excavate the entire lost city. Attending to the time and space around the lines is not so much adding or creating as it is uncovering what is already there, waiting to be revealed. Directing is archeological.

While the typographic space between two lines on the page will always be the same width, the director should understand that space as variable and flexible. Sometimes the director needs to contribute only the most minuscule detail in that space. Other times he may need to insert three whole minutes of material, as my example above suggests. As much as possible, try not to let time dictate your work. Do not worry about things around the lines being too busy or taking too long. Worry instead about creating the conditions necessary to make each line absolutely essential. Make believability your measuring stick, not the clock. Watch the work, and if a line is spoken without reason, stop and get out your tools and build whatever bridge, whatever scaffold is necessary to credibly reach that line. Do not accept even one line uttered without justification.

You can ask actors to collaborate with you in this effort by inviting them to explore around the lines, too. One of the best ways of doing this is to encourage them to take all the time they need. Time is among the most generous gifts you can give an actor, especially when they are working on a long monologue. Human beings don't speak in monologues. We speak one line at a time. Almost never in life—unless we are reading something scripted—do we know in advance that we will speak a monologue. If an actor approaches Hamlet's "To be or not to be" speech as a monologue, she is doomed. She needs instead to imagine the speech does not exist—once again, the idea of there being no text—and locate the need to speak each and every line. We can support actors in this rigorous pursuit by not rushing them or allowing them to rush themselves. I call this deliberate slowing down *waiting for the text*, a simple technique and reminder for actors to search for the need to speak rather than assuming that need already exists.

The title and main idea of this essay also remind us that plays are not literature. So-called classics of the dramatic canon, such as **A Streetcar Named Desire** and **Death of a Salesman**, are routinely taught in literature classes and subjected to literary analysis applied to novels. This highlights an unfortunate misunderstanding. Literature is a closed and finished medium. When a book is published, it is a complete artwork. But a play is only an invitation to an artwork that might be completed at some later date. A single play can generate a million different productions, where a book can only ever be itself. Plays are like architectural drawings or recipes—delightful to pore over and worth studying, but only from the perspective of what they might eventually yield. It is a mistake to collect and display plays on bookshelves as if they are finished. They should rather be kept perpetually in the workshop, out in the garage, always open to some page, always surrounded by tools and construction.

Speaking of which, let's return to our tower of lines, which I hope is still standing! Earlier I suggested how we could build up the space before Medvedenko's first line, "Why do you always wear mourning?" Let's turn our attention now to the next line of the scene. Pull it off the top of the tower and place it on your desk next to the first line, leaving a bit of space between like this:

Medvedenko Why do you always wear mourning?

Masha I dress in black to match my life. I am unhappy.

By now you know that little space between the lines is your zone, the place where you must make something happen, even if it is so small as to barely deserve mention. Even if it is just Masha throwing a glance in Medvedenko's direction or adjusting her sunglasses. Or breathing in to steady herself against the undeniable challenges she is facing in life and love. What will it be? What will let the actress playing Masha speak these words as if nothing else could ever be said?

The choice is yours.

An epidemic of talking is underway in theatre rehearsal rooms. It is happening before rehearsal begins, in lieu of actors warming up and centering themselves. It is happening during the initial **table work** sessions that launch most rehearsal processes. It is happening in the middle of staging rehearsals and sessions that had been intended for movement work or physical exploration. Sometimes the director initiates the talking, sometimes the actor initiates it, and sometimes another team member initiates it like the stage manager or dramaturg. Regardless of who starts it the basic effect of talking, on the talker and those around him, is always the same: talking activates our intellectual centers of analysis and perception—the head—and deactivates our instinctive and emotional centers—the heart. Talking does not turn off the heart completely, but it turns it down. You cannot send attention and energy to one center without stealing them from the other.

The opposite of talking is *doing*. In rehearsals, doing involves speaking the lines of the play, performing its actions, or conducting embodied exploration of the world of the play through physical exercises or improvisations. Doing means these investigations are being carried out without discussion. Doing is about existing within rather than commenting upon. Actors are sometimes praised for "staying in the moment," which is just another way of describing doing. Actors who stay in the moment, and directors who assist them in attaining and sustaining that state, are practicing doing. Staying in the moment is staying in the doing. By definition, analysis is retrospective. Talking fixes our attention on the past. Doing, on the other hand, is firmly rooted in the present. This distinction is profound for directors and actors seeking authenticity and spontaneity in their work.

Both talking and doing have their place in creative process, and it is not my intention to suggest that talking be completely eliminated from rehearsal. Sometimes talking is very important. **Intimacy direction**, **fight choreography**, or staging that is physically or technically complex are all instances in a rehearsal process where talking and discussion are essential. Talking is warranted whenever safety is a legitimate concern. Directors are caretakers, and we must prioritize safety and the communication required to ensure it. But elsewhere in the rehearsal process, where safety is not on the line, we can afford to reduce our talking. If exploration is our goal and doing is the most committed way of accomplishing that goal, why are we still so prone to talking? One reason is that talking just feels easier, and that ease is attractive to us. Our animal instincts, hard-wired to conserve energy and protect against overexertion, recognize that moving the mouth requires less effort than engaging the body and imagination. At other times, however, our decision to talk stems from a much deeper concern: the fear of losing control of ourselves.

Talking instantly assuages this fear, halting exploration into the unknown world of the play and depositing us back into familiar, reassuring surroundings. We come tumbling back to ourselves. Talking halts any transformation the actor might have been undergoing into a character. If they had kept going, if they had kept doing, they might have found themselves occupying a new body, and understandably, that may be disorienting and even frightening. At the same time, transformation lies at the heart of what actors do and what directors facilitate. Transformation into another self is what separates acting from lecturing or public speaking, for instance. Acting is not a presentation of character but a committed embodiment of it, and to direct is to gently guide actors in this alchemy.

Interrupting exploration of the play with talking is like pulling the rehearsal over to the side of the road. The longer your pit stop, the harder it is to get back on the road and to remember why you set out on the journey in the first place. It's a shame actors can't manage talking and doing at the same time, but alas, it is difficult if not impossible, as any director has realized when trying to carry on a conversation with an actor who is rehearsing onstage. Attempting talking and doing simultaneously can result in real confusion or even chaos that may be harmful to the actor. Talking and doing are best undertaken separately when rehearsing a play, and as the leader of the rehearsal process, the director is primarily responsible for deciding how talking and doing will be balanced. I have observed many rehearsal rooms where the ratio of talking to doing is about three to one—that is,

75 percent talking and 25 percent doing. Directors would do well to at least balance these forces, and in the best of all worlds, the ratio would be flipped, with three-quarters of your time spent on doing. This comes with the caveat that on any given day, actors should feel free not to undertake transformation, and it is essential that directors communicate to actors they have this right. Actors are always free to step out of the work if they are confused or uncomfortable, and whenever they do, it is a signal to the director that talking would be helpful.

We must acknowledge that intellectual analysis and thoughtful discussion can offer insights into plays and other works of art. Education, after all, is founded upon analysis and discussion. But rehearsing a play is not primarily about education. Though any healthy rehearsal process will spark learning, the learning will be more experiential than intellectual. Rehearsing a play is more about feeling the play, learning to connect to it, than analyzing it. We directors seek to empathize with the characters and world of a play, and to inspire the same empathy in our actors. We seek this empathy on a deep, molecular level, inviting our own atoms to vibrate for a time at new frequencies. It is far easier to approach these physical adjustments through doing than talking. Talking about transformation only distances one from the site and experience of it. Talking about transformation objectifies it, declaring it something other than, and outside of, oneself. *Talking about transformation is a retreat from transformation.* There is a fascinating corollary here to a principle in physics called the observer effect, which states that attempting to observe and measure an object always alters the object itself, since the measurement process and the instruments required inevitably disturb the object in some way, even if that disturbance is very small. A common example of the observer effect is checking tire pressure. In taking a pressure reading, a little air is always lost, and you will never be able to know what the precise pressure was before you started taking the reading. Continuing to check the tires will result in even more lost air. The more we try to pin down a profound experience, the further we drift from the experience itself, risking ever more approximation in our description.

If your actors and other collaborators are particularly prone to talking over doing, you can employ some gentle strategies to reverse this. Explain to the team that you wish to rehearse scenes without stopping, and ask them to hold any questions they may have (unless personal safety is at risk) until the scene is over. If you frequently interject your own notes and comments into the rehearsal, challenge yourself to give those notes later in the day—or at the end of the session. You might find that a note resolves itself without your interference. If your notes and comments tend toward the verbose, streamline them to the bare essentials. Promote doing at the top of rehearsals by starting with movement work or a vigorous warm-up rather than discussion, and break up sedentary stretches of the rehearsal process, such as table work, with exercises and games that engage the body. Do not ever allow actors to sit for more than an hour. When you encounter what feels like a roadblock in a scene, rather than stopping to discuss and dissect, make the radical choice instead to try one more time, to push a little further. The moments where we most want to stop are often moments on the threshold of a breakthrough. Sensing that transformation is imminent, we become shy, tired, and reluctant to proceed. These are the moments when the doing becomes vital, to coax ourselves beyond ourselves so we may tumble into the light.

You will find that some phases of your rehearsal process gravitate more toward talking than others. Table work, the first phase of most rehearsal processes where the director and actors gather around a table to begin working together, is one such place. Admittedly, it is hard to leap into doing when we are just meeting each other. Still, we can endeavor to keep the talking as productive as possible. All too often, talking during table work veers into speculation that cannot be substantiated by the play. Directors should be firm in insisting that discussion remain within the boundaries of the play, as the playwright has prescribed them. While it may be amusing for actors and directors to dream up vivid backstories and past intrigues for the characters, ultimately we are wasting our time if our imaginations lead us into territory that cannot be verified in the play. The purpose of table work discussions should be to get everyone on the same page about the world of the play and the story being told, and we should not stray further than that. For example, during table work for the *The Seagull*, it would be sensible to discuss the lack of a father figure in Konstantin's life and the impact this can have on a child or adolescent, since this detail of Konstantin's biography surfaces in several scenes of the play. But it would be a waste of time to speculate about who Konstantin's father was, when he departed the boy's life, or whether Konstantin or his mother have ever seen him again. These questions might inspire a juicy prequel to *The Seagull*, should someone wish to write one, but they have no place in a group rehearsal of the play because they are ultimately unverifiable in the play itself. If the actor playing Konstantin wishes to meditate on these questions on his own time, that is of course his prerogative.

This is not to discourage imagination in the rehearsal process. In fact, there will be many times where you and your team will need to engage the imagination to fill in gaps in the world of the play. A lake is referred to many times in *The Seagull*, but the play offers no concrete description of the lake. Is the lake large or small, choppy or calm, unpeopled or active with fishing, boating, and other human activity? The play answers none of these questions definitively, yet they will be important to answer as part of the rehearsal process, so that the actors have a complete portrait of the setting. You and the actors will need to engage your imaginations to answer these questions. However, as you do, it is imperative you work from what the play has given you. Noting Arkadina's description in Act One of the parties they used to see on the opposite shore, you might conclude the lake is not entirely secluded and that other locals are seen from time to time. Medevedenko's description in Act Four of the wind whipping off the lake, combined with some research into weather patterns around lakes, might help you conclude this is at least a moderate-sized lake. We engage our imaginations to fill in critical gaps in the world of the play already provided to us, not to build new worlds. The role of the imagination in the rehearsal process is to clarify and complete, not to invent. When the imagining goes too far, it is the director's job to rein it in.

Acting is the pursuit of an objective through actions. Actions may be psychological or physical. Psychological actions are internal and driven by the mind and intellect, such as teaching, convincing, criticizing, praising, and pleading. Physical actions are external and driven by the body, such as running, jumping, lifting, singing, and calling.

One of your most important jobs as a director is to ensure actors really do actions rather than pretend to do them. For instance, when a play calls for drinking fluid, actors in rehearsal have a habit of miming drinking rather than actually consuming fluid, and directors have a habit of letting them get away with it. While this may eliminate some clean-up after the rehearsal, it also, unfortunately, makes the actor's action look and feel false. Give the actor real fluid to drink—simple water will do—and their drinking instantly becomes more believable. When you do not believe an action on stage, you must call it out and repair it. Proceed with care, bearing in mind how vulnerable reality is for actors in a play. To do an action for real in the shoes of a character is an acknowledgment of transformation. The more extreme the character and the character's actions, the more dangerous it feels to do things for real. There is great temptation to fake even the most mundane actions of **Macbeth** or **Stanley Kowalski**.

Actions can be brief or go on for quite some time, especially if the character's objective is challenging. An action performed in a play should take the same amount of time that it would take in real life. Actors and directors are content to follow this rule when an action is quick, but they hesitate to give lengthy actions their full due. They worry about taking too long or boring the audience, haunted by memories of past directors or producers enjoining them to "Cut the pauses!" or "Pick up the pace!" Yet abbreviating an action leads to approximation, a sketched version that convinces no one. Advise the actor instead to slow down and elongate the action, letting it run its natural course. If the scene calls for an actor to knock with concern on a door, and in his first rehearsal of the scene he knocks for just two seconds, make him knock again for five. If he accepts that, make him knock again for ten. If he accepts that, make him knock for thirty seconds. Knocking on a door for thirty seconds demands more physical and emotional commitment than knocking on a door for two seconds. The extra effort required makes it harder for the actor to pretend the action, compelling him toward authenticity.

Sometimes you will want to intensify an actor's commitment to an action without making it take longer. You will simply want to ask the actor to do the action with more energy and engagement. But this can be challenging, especially when it comes to psychological actions, since they are so internal and intangible. You can assist actors in intensifying psychological actions by pairing them with physical actions. For example, if the actor's character is *convincing* another character of something, you can also ask the actor to lean across the table, stand up rapidly, raise her voice, pound the tabletop emphatically, or reach across the table and take the other character's hand imploringly—provided the actor across the table has been forewarned and consents. These are just a few of the many possible physical actions you might graft upon the psychological action of convincing. They provide the actor a simple physical behavior that she can focus on intensifying during the course of the scene. The intensification of the physical action will usually result in a simultaneous intensification of the psychological action—as the actor raises her voice or pounds the table harder, her convincing becomes more impassioned.

Occasionally, you will ask actors to intensify an action, and they will respond they are already playing it to the fullest extent possible. This issue most often arises around psychological actions. The actor contends he is doing all he can, but the director is not feeling or seeing enough. The actor needs help with allowing his internal work to radiate outward. This process is called *externalization.* All actions, but especially psychological ones, must ultimately create patterns of behavior that an outside observer can detect and understand. The first recourse here is simply to explain to the actor that you are not yet seeing enough on the outside and to ask him if he can show more. If that fails to produce results and the action remains stubbornly internalized, work with the actor to incorporate a physical action, as described above. This can unlock and enliven the body, coaxing the internal action out into view. It can be humbling for an actor to feel like he is trying his best but still not delivering. Be patient and gentle, reassuring him that you are his ally in making the character and story as clear as possible.

An actor may play a dozen or more actions in a scene, and all must be done for real. When an actor struggles to achieve authenticity with multiple actions in a scene, or if the entire scene feels unconvincing or lacking in intensity, it suggests the actor is having trouble relating to the circumstances of the scene. A tool to utilize in this situation is the *magic if*. First articulated by Stanislavski in his formulation of modern acting technique, the *magic if* works by substitution, inviting an actor to call upon his own life experience in moments where his character or the play feel foreign. In Anton Chekhov's *Three Sisters*, three young women feel depressed and isolated in a rural Russian military community and desperately wish to return to their urban lives in the cosmopolitan city of Moscow. While these exact circumstances will be unfamiliar to most actors, an actor could say the women's isolation is *as if* they were living through a Covid-19 lockdown and unable to leave home or meet any of their friends—circumstances the actor can readily relate to.

The *magic if* should never be employed to gratuitously dredge up an actor's past. It is a spot treatment to be used sparingly and judiciously, and it should be discarded once the actor's grasp of the character's circumstances has been strengthened. At the same time, do not hesitate to use the *magic if* when you need it. There is no weakness in doing so. Its very existence as a tool reminds us that actors are not expected to immediately connect to, much less directly possess, life experiences equal to their character's. The *magic if* allows an actor to play Trigorin in *The Seagull* even if he has not been a famous writer, and to play Shakespeare's Romeo even if she has never scaled the garden wall of her parents' mortal enemy to flirt with her lover on a balcony. There is an important exception however. Where accurate and respectful representation is a concern, such as with characters with disabilities, it is not appropriate to use the *magic if* or any other method of substitution. Characters with disabilities should always be played by actors with their own lived experience with disability.

Challenging actors toward greater authenticity may amplify the level of conflict in the scene. Do not be alarmed by this. It's a good thing, as conflict is an essential ingredient in drama. Plays begin in equilibrium and progress to turbulence, and characters are constantly in some form of conflict or competition with each other. The conflict between them doesn't always take the form of a fist fight or screaming match, but as a general rule, every character wants something from every other character at all times. Plays are not written about ordinary people or ordinary days. Plays with a veneer of normalcy and stasis, like Chekhov's plays, mask waves of turmoil just below their surface. You should feel free to speak openly with actors about the conflict in a scene, and you should not hesitate to ask them to intensify the level of conflict, so long as they can do it safely and you feel the play warrants it. Conflict has become a dirty word, and understandably so, given the heartbreaking divisions lately in our world. To be clear, I am in no way endorsing conflict in the rehearsal process itself. The rehearsal process, and the rehearsal room, must be suffused with kindness and care at all times. But within the fictional world of the play, I am advocating for the relationships between the characters to be fiery, passionate, and deeply contentious. Otherwise the drama will not be sustained, and the play will deflate like a balloon.

When we strip scenes of conflict or allow the actors to underplay it, we effectively authorize a distortion of the story we had agreed to tell. Something similar happens when we water down, or perhaps even cut, acts of violence in a play. We should never feel obligated to stage a play that contains violence. But if we do decide to stage such a play, we must present its full truth, embodying even the play's most uncomfortable dimensions. As we do, it is essential we incorporate into the rehearsal process additional support personnel and resources to monitor the well-being of the entire creative team. Additional personnel could include intimacy coordinators, fight choreographers, and even counselors or mental health professionals. It is the director's responsibility to tread carefully around difficult and potentially traumatizing material, recognizing the toll it can take on everyone in the rehearsal room, including the director herself. Rehearsals of potentially upsetting material are times in the process when talking may be more appropriate than doing. The director should make it abundantly clear to actors that they may halt the work at any time. We must distinguish the weight of our subject matter, which may be heavy indeed, from the creative process itself, which should be buoyant and light. The making of theatre must always be a joy, a celebration, a party, and if we cannot ensure it will be those things for us and our team, we should take a break. We should leave the rehearsal room until we are ready to party again.

Sharpening the edges of conflict in a scene can initially result in rehearsals where the actors appear to be straining, or as some like to call it, *pushing*. Pushing makes some directors and teachers—especially those whose techniques are grounded in relaxation—very uncomfortable. Clearly, any strain that threatens the physical well-being of the actor must be curtailed immediately. But pushing that is not harmful and that is merely clumsy or ungainly should be allowed to continue, since it is the result of exploration, and exploration is essential to rehearsal. What bothers people about pushing is not so much the strain of it as the mess it creates. We have a nasty habit of demanding the work be cleaned up before it has even begun, and we need to practice being more tolerant of disorder, reminding ourselves that ideas rarely tumble into the world fully mature and grown-up.

Gently and respectfully, resist those who urge you to tidy and organize prematurely. Asking a director to make a rehearsal process clean is like asking a painter never to drip a bit of paint on the floor, or a carpenter never to throw sawdust into the air. Making art is messy because making art involves combination and transformation. Though theatre does not work with physical mediums and tools in the same way other arts do, theatre must be allowed to drip its paint on the floor, too. Resist cleaning up as long as you can, as long as the work in your judgment remains safe and productive. This is not a license to be reckless. Directors should never set out to break or destroy. You must treat the rehearsal room, and everyone and everything in it, with respect. Do not unduly burden anyone with cleaning up after you. You may need to roll up your sleeves and mop the floor, but don't let this limit your experiments. Mess is like the space sweating. A messy space is a sign that the play got a good workout. If the rehearsal can be cleaned up in two minutes, you and the team didn't work hard enough. Mess and disorder are part of the creative process.

We tolerate mess more from artists working in other mediums, such as painting, sculpture, and installation, than we do from artists working in theatre. In the visual arts, there is the concept of the artist's studio, a place where multiple projects may be seen in various stages of completion. The medium—the painter's paint or the sculptor's clay—may be visible alongside works that are finished and ready to be displayed in the gallery. Process and product are nestled together. Obviously, there are differences between the visual artist's studio and the rehearsal room, namely that the studio is private and belongs to just one artist, while the rehearsal room is shared with your entire team—and perhaps even other theatre companies. The visual artist is an owner, while the theatre artist is a renter. But despite these differences, you can still embrace the ethos of the artist's studio in your rehearsal room.

For a long time, I struggled to invite mess into my creative space. Eventually, I began to understand the word itself may be unhelpful and off-putting. A better word for mess is "process." We might think of mess as a willingness to celebrate process over product, a gratitude for the beauty of something as it takes root without worrying about its future shape or meaning, or what it will look like tomorrow, or how long it will endure. Process snaps us into the present. It is joyous and life-affirming, and even as a production moves toward completion, we can retain an element of process by leaving some of our tools still scattered about the space, unmasked and unhidden, plainly in view for the audience to see. There is a great deal of discussion about creating safe spaces, but not enough focus on the role process plays in establishing such spaces. [Embracing process and mess fosters a safe and productive rehearsal environment by signaling that expression, not perfection, is the goal.] People feel free to play rather than pressured to get things right.

Achieving authenticity frequently demands more exploration and exertion than we initially thought was required. This goes as much for directors as it does for actors. **Peter Brook** described exhaustion as the most important tool in rehearsal. While setting out purely to exhaust ourselves is masochistic and unnecessary, effort and sweat can be reliable indications that productive work is underway. There is a myth of effortlessness surrounding art and performance. People mistakenly correlate artistic success with ease, asserting that the best work is accomplished with the least effort, and that the best ideas fall out of the sky. That may happen once or twice, but mostly, directing is hard work and should feel like it. If you are coasting through rehearsal after rehearsal, without feeling tested or challenged, it is a sure sign you can do more. You need to get real.

Directing is a process of seeing more and more each day. You are certain you are seeing the entire landscape of the play, then the next day, you discover something wonderful and new you had never seen before, the layers of the play peeling back a little further. This discovery does not mean you were careless in your observations the day before. It just highlights how the depth and clarity of our directorial vision increases over time. But none of us can see everything. Our vision will never be complete without the observations of others. We give criticism as directors, but we desperately need to receive it, too. It can be challenging, however, to distinguish constructive criticism from the less helpful, and sometimes even destructive, variety.

For criticism to be worth your time and consideration, it should meet two criteria. First, it needs to clearly explain its reasoning and position in a manner that is accessible to you. Second, it must offer a solution—once again, in terms you understand—for fixing the problem. Many critics excel at pointing out what they perceive to be flaws in a performance; far fewer offer coherent suggestions for revision. Some critics will surely disagree with me on this, insisting their job stops at the diagnosis. Respectfully, I disagree. What sense is a diagnosis without an accompanying proposal of treatment, of care? Calling something out without a plan for making it right is too easy. Ultimately all worthwhile criticism should be more invested in development than demolition.

As Bruno Latour writes in his essay, "Why has Critique Run out of Steam? From Matters of Fact to Matters of Concern," "The critic is not the one who debunks, but the one who assembles. The critic is not the one who lifts the rugs from under the feet of the naïve believers, but the one who offers the participants arenas in which to gather. The critic is . . . the one for whom, if something is constructed, then it means it is fragile and thus in great need of care and caution."

Even when a director receives constructive criticism, it may still be hard for him to hear and absorb. Directors have a bad habit of resisting good notes, and if you feel this sort of resistance bubbling up in yourself, stop and try to identify its cause. Sometimes it is simply our passion and pride getting in the way: we love our ideas and are reluctant to see them from someone else's perspective. Other times it is an issue of trust. We reject the note, despite its merits, because we are unfamiliar with the source. If you can recognize that a note is constructive and that you would have immediately taken it, had it come from a trusted friend or colleague, entertain the notion that this helpful critic might well be on the way to becoming your friend, for their heart seems to be in the right place. Give their note a try. Perhaps the most insidious cause of dismissing a good note is a fear of showing weakness. Mindful of the leadership role we play in the rehearsal process, we hesitate to change course for fear of suggesting that we are lost, or even worse, that we are wrong. Our anxiousness to be seen as right has been fueled by the pervasive myth of the director as omniscient and omnipotent. In this myth, the director regales his team with one brilliant idea after another, exhibits unflappable confidence and certainty at every turn, and on the very rare occasion the production runs into trouble, he retreats to the corner to brood in silence before returning to the group, savior-like, with a prescription for rescuing the rehearsal.

It is high time we revised that image because times have changed. The auteur is dead. The solitary genius is dead, at least when it comes to directors. These tropes are outdated and absurd in the midst of our refreshing conversations around decentering power and democratizing creative space. There is nothing but buffoonery today in the image of the director as a master, ensconced behind his rehearsal table and stroking his beard, the rest of the team holding their breath until he graces them with his next epiphany. Nothing today suggests that anyone is waiting on the director anymore. On the contrary, what is emerging is a revised image of the director serving everyone else. Far from aloof, the director today is radically social, a champion of inclusion and collaboration at every turn in the creative process. The director today facilitates as much as he articulates. He uses his status as a leader to foster and maintain the conditions in which great impulses may emerge— occasionally from himself, but more often from those around him. He opens himself to the intelligence of others, acting as a vessel through which the energy and brilliance of his collaborators may surge into the work. The director today is humbler, quieter, and gentler than he has ever been. These are signs of progress, not diminutions of the position, as some old-timers would have you think. Today you can feel free to say you do not know. Today you can feel free to say, "I would like to do whatever is best for you." Today you can embrace the advice of others, celebrating the sophistication and maturity you demonstrate in doing so. Today it is the director who insists on going it alone who looks silly. Don't be him.

When you direct in a place that is foreign to you—not just geographically but perhaps also socially, culturally, or politically—it becomes nearly impossible to avoid opening yourself to others' ideas, at least to some degree. For this reason *directing out of town*, if you have the chance to do it, is like a tonic for your directing. I have been directing in Romania for more than a decade. I do not speak Romanian or Hungarian, the languages in which my productions are presented there, and while many of the actors with whom I work speak some English, I insist on translators always being present in rehearsal. This may sound like a complicated process, but it is actually a privilege, encouraging me to lean into nonverbal elements of theatrical storytelling—light, sound, gesture, time, space—that I tend to underutilize when directing in the United States, where I am surrounded by others who speak and think like me. Directing in unfamiliar surroundings forces me, in the most positive sense, to innovate, to stretch myself creatively, as I search for respectful ways to bridge the gaps between my ideas and those of my collaborators. Directing out of town puts me in a controlled crisis that challenges my own basic assumptions about how and why I make art. Directing out of town is a deliberate self-disruption, an entreaty to myself to edge out of my comfort zone.

Directing out of town can feel like you are doing everything all wrong and directing for the very first time, and in that way, it is an exercise in humility and patience like no other. Directing out of town carries serious risk of failure, but also serious potential for growth. Getting things right all the time only reinforces what you already know. It doesn't expand your vision or your vocabulary. I recognize that failure is a hard pill to swallow, with the pressure you may feel to succeed, with the time and money you may be devoting to your training or your career. But if you can invite the possibility of failure into your creative process, even just a little, your directing will leap forward. Every failure now is one less mistake you will make down the road. Errors today become tools tomorrow.

Directing out of town does not necessarily mean traveling far. Just working in another neighborhood, or with another school, or with a new community partner, may be enough to make it feel like you have left home. Simply put, directing out of town happens whenever we collaborate with others who live and create differently from us. Artists have long stressed the importance of nurturing partnerships and building up networks of colleagues, but these practices can also lead to insularity, where we are making our work, and sharing it, with the same coterie over and over again. We do need long-term artistic relationships from which to draw love and support, but surrounding ourselves exclusively with people who share our impulses and ideas can make our directing stale.

Directing out of town challenges us to do things someone else's way, messes up our routines, pushes us to locate new sensations and anatomies, and all this disruption can be wildly inspirational. It asks us to adapt and repattern, especially if working with artists whose practices lie outside the traditional boundaries of theatre, such as filmmakers, dancers, sculptors, painters, poets, or musicians. Multidisciplinary collaborations require that we devise a new language together, a hybrid artistic tongue that is specific and unique to the project at hand. Years ago, I began collaborating with a Hungarian violinist named János. Together we made multidisciplinary works at the intersection of theatre, installation, and experimental music. In addition to being a wonderful musician, János was also a wonderful storyteller, and he loved to tell a story about when he first arrived in Switzerland, after fleeing Budapest during the Hungarian Revolution in 1956.

There János was, sitting on a bench in a park in Zürich. Though it was a private and lovely spot on a little path, tucked in a grove of trees, János still felt rather blue. The romanticism of fleeing to the West had worn off. He had no food or place to stay, and not a cent to his name, having just spent the last of his money on a pack of cigarettes. He had nothing of value except for his violin in a battered case at his feet.

But I might as well be dead without my instrument, he thought, I can't possibly part with that.

For all intents and purposes, the pack of cigarettes was his last earthly possession, and he was smoking through it pretty fast. Once he finished, he had no idea what would happen next. But he figured it couldn't be good. János felt like this might be the end of the line.

He sat and smoked, and when he arrived at the last cigarette, he twirled it consequentially in his fingers.

I guess this is it, he thought.

Just as he lit that last cigarette, its tip blazing red like a warning or a flare, a stranger strolled up the path now dappled in the afternoon sun. He was a fellow of indeterminate age, in a suit of indeterminate gray—not quite silver, not quite charcoal, but something shimmering in between, like fog in the wind or light upon the water.

Can you spare a cigarette? he asked János.

Knowing he could spare neither that nor anything else, János promptly burst into tears, telling the stranger everything about his sorry state and situation. The stranger listened quietly without interrupting, only nodding now and then. Later János would realize he had babbled everything out in Hungarian, a wickedly unspeakable tongue unless you happen to be

Hungarian, which János figured the stranger was not. But the stranger's miraculous comprehension did not register with János in the moment, overcome as he was.

János reached the end of his story, took a last drag on the little nub left in his fingers, and flicked it to the ground. There was nothing left to smoke and nothing left to say. The stranger sat down then next to János—until then he had been standing—and gazed down the path to where the trees swallowed it up. His eyes wandered to the violin at János' feet.

Who did you say your teacher is again? the stranger asked.

I don't have a teacher, János sighed. How could I afford a teacher?

That's right, the stranger said, gazing back down the path.

Then he pulled a checkbook from his pocket and wrote János a check for 500 Swiss Francs— something on the order of $5,000 today. The stranger smiled, put a hand on János' shoulder, and without another word, disappeared down the path, leaving János stunned and speechless, weeping once again.

To work with János was to be immersed in stories like this every day. They flowed effortlessly and endlessly from him, over lunch, on a coffee break, so that my impression of the world after a day's rehearsal with János was one of charity and warmth, where those with means helped those without them, and where art was the undying flower refusing to be trampled upon, refusing to be stamped out. What I never told János directly, though I am sure he sensed it, was how much I needed these stories. We began working together during a period of intense personal doubt, when I had made up my mind—or so I thought—to leave theatre. My heart was no longer in it. I began the project with János thinking it would be one of my last. But all it made me do was fall in love with theatre again.

János and I made three performances before he passed while undergoing surgery for a blood clot. I treasure the art we made together, but I treasure our friendship and his stories even more. I miss him dearly and still feel his loss. He will always be a reminder to me of how the best ideas may lie well beyond ourselves, in another place, in another country even, but above all, in another person.

Have you ever come back to a moment you were directing in rehearsal the previous day—a moment you loved, that you thought was working great—and found that now you can't stand it? Have you ever gone to a second performance of your production and found yourself inexplicably disappointed, even though everything appears to be working as it should? What is going on in these instances? The element of surprise is absent. This is a frustrating, disorienting feeling, but rest assured that every director has felt it since the dawn of directorial time.

Revisiting a moment you have already directed, you can admire what you made, and you can relish the memory of making it. But you will never recover the pure rush of excitement you felt when you first invented the moment. Seeing the moment again, you will always experience it as something less-than-before. Keeping this in mind can help you manage your expectations. At the same time, if the disappointment is too bitter, you should have some technical means for restoring surprise to your work. Here are three tools for accomplishing this:

1. Do the Opposite. However you have directed an action thus far, however an actor has been playing it, do the opposite. Do not merely adjust the action but rather do a full 180-degree about-face of it. If the actor has been *pleading*, ask him now to *dismiss*. If the actor has been *running*, ask him to *stand still*. If the actor has been *criticizing*, ask him now to *praise*. Do the Opposite is the simplest and most straightforward surprise-generating tool, and it is easy to employ: you just turn around and run as hard as you can in the other direction. There is no intellectual analysis required beyond considering for a split second what the opposite action is. But do not consider for too long, as delaying dulls the effect of the surprise.

While the scene is being rehearsed, the director can call out, "Do the Opposite," provided the actors are familiar with the tool. (It is never wise to use a tool or technique in the rehearsal room without having first explained it.) The actor's action will suddenly change, introducing a jolt of new behavior into the scene. It is important to emphasize that the actor's objective—and of course the text itself—should remain unchanged. Do the Opposite is a radical adjustment of action only. Generally, the actor should continue doing the opposite for as long as the new action remains interesting and does not obstruct her character's objective.

For example, let's say a character's objective is to finish a chapter for a book as soon as possible. She is writing furiously, hunched over her notebook at a desk. She is a picture of intense concentration. Then the director instructs her to Do the Opposite. She stops writing, gazes out the window, and whistles a carefree tune. This sudden change of action is exciting and intriguing. It accomplishes our directorial goal of sparking new behavior in the scene. But eventually, in order to continue pursuing her objective, the character will need to take up her pen again and resume writing. There is no way that continuing to stare out the window, whistling a tune, will get the chapter done—if only this were the case!

Do the Opposite ends with the actor reverting to what she was doing before the tool was used—or some action very much like it. It results in only a *temporary* adjustment of action. But in the process, we have sparked new material in the scene, lifting our creative spirits. We also may have discovered a pattern of behavior for the character that could work elsewhere in the play.

2. The Left Turn. The Left Turn is an abrupt change that *permanently* alters the actor's action. Once again, the actor may not change his objective, but he adopts an entirely different course of action for accomplishing it, abandoning his previous approach. A Left Turn is like finding a new, unexpected route of ascent up the mountain and never looking back.

Let's say you have discovered the joys of sourdough bread-making and you want to get your friend excited about bread-making, too, so that he will bake with you next time. You would like some company. To accomplish this objective, you gleefully start describing the process, pointing to the tools and ingredients you have set on your counter as visual aids. If you were a character in a play, your main action would be *explaining*, for the bread-making process is completely new to your friend. You describe how to mix the ingredients; how to fold the dough every half hour for the first three hours; how to judge by the dough's increased volume that bulk fermentation is complete; how to divide the dough; how to proof the dough; and how all these steps are dependent on the time of year and temperature of your kitchen. You love talking about this stuff, but you notice your friend's eyes glazing over. He seems uninterested, and it is clear you are not accomplishing your objective of getting him excited about baking. You decide to abruptly change course, ceasing your action of *explaining* and instead *dazzling* your friend with the bread itself! You say, "Why don't we just have a slice!" You take the sourdough loaf, which had been cooling on a rack behind you, and place it on a rustic wooden cutting board. You pause over the loaf for a moment, admiring the concentric rings of flour on its surface, and you can feel your friend admiring them, too. "Beautiful," you say, slicing into the bread slowly, steam dancing out. You scrape butter and homemade jam across the surface of the slice, letting them melt into its crags and airy holes, and then you slide the slice over to your friend. "Try it," you say, with a smile. He does and sighs with delight.

"It's delicious," he says. "Let's bake a loaf right now. Put me to work!"

Although the example I provide here is not from a play or rehearsal situation, it illustrates how Left Turns introduce a surprising new course of action that energizes and enlivens both the person doing the action, as well as his scene partner. A Left Turn is sharp but never gratuitous. It is a way for an actor to try something radically new in rehearsal when the actor's current course of action feels stale or exhausted. It immediately introduces new behavior into the scene, provoking surprise. Left

Turns aren't just about finding variety in action—something many directors and actors speak of. They are about *making a wildly, radically different choice*, and doing so in the least predictable manner possible. They are a swerve and a dive down a new path.

Imagine the famous balcony scene from Shakespeare's *Romeo and Juliet*. The actors playing the two lovers are staring at each other, Juliet above from her balcony and Romeo from the garden below. The actor playing Romeo has an objective of *getting Juliet to recognize and appreciate his affections for her*. The actor playing Romeo is doing actions like *complimenting* and *flirting*, but as the scene drags on, the actor feels uninspired in these actions. He feels he is not achieving his character's objective. Suddenly, at the director's encouragement, he tries a Left Turn, something he has never done before in rehearsal. He delivers his line, "O, wilt though leave me so unsatisfied?" And then, before Juliet can reply, Romeo goes into a full-on headstand, an impressive feat! Juliet, surprised and amused, laughs as she inquires of this man, standing on his head for her, "What satisfaction canst though have tonight?" "The exchange of thy love's faithful vow for mine," Romeo says, flipping back to standing with a flourish and a little bow. Juliet—or perhaps the actress playing Juliet—can't help but applaud for a moment before the two carry on with the scene that has been invigorated by Romeo's unexpected display of physical playfulness and prowess.

For maximum effect, use Do the Opposite spontaneously, to generate surprise on the spur of the moment. Left Turns, on the other hand, ought to be prepared in advance, after completing a standard analysis of a scene's actions and objectives. If done correctly, your analysis will have set out logical progressions of actions for the characters to play in pursuing their objectives. Identify a few spots where you feel it would be interesting to disrupt these progressions with Left Turns. Try these in rehearsal.

Surprise nourishes actors, too, and if you take the time to orient actors to these tools, most of them will appreciate their value. Some actors may be slower to accept them, however, especially if their technique is rooted in control. Be ready if challenged to gently explain why you feel a scene needs surprise—this would be an instance when stopping to talk would be warranted. It may help to anchor your justification of these tools in the observation that human beings are both deliberate and unpredictable. In real life, we are surprised every day, and tools like Do the Opposite and The Left Turn provide technical means for replicating the spontaneity of life in the rehearsal process.

3. The Postmodern Choice. Before moving on to this third surprise-generating tool, let's pause for a bit of background. You may have heard the term *postmodernism* before, but if not, don't worry. Tracing the complete history and meaning of the term is beyond the scope of this book. For our purposes it is enough to say that postmodernism is an artistic movement characterized by a mixture of styles, genres, and methods. Postmodern art makes room for both the classical and the contemporary to coexist. Modernism prioritizes unity and consistency of style; if someone tells you they want everything in a room to match nicely, they are thinking in a modernist way. Postmodernism, on the other hand, deliberately rejects unity, reveling in incongruities and juxtapositions ranging from the amusing to the profane.

Postmodernism deserves the attention of directors for three big reasons. First, beginning in the mid-1960s, it influenced a slew of experimental and avant-garde directors whose work continues to inspire contemporary theatre-making practices today. These directors, who included **Elizabeth LeCompte**, **Richard Schechner**, **Judith Malina**, **Julian Beck**, **Joseph Chaikin**, **Joanne Akalaitis**, and **Lee Breuer**, are all worth studying for their multidisciplinary, socially engaged theatre. Second, as an aesthetic mashup, postmodernism resembles the media-saturated world we live in today. Finally, when it emerged, postmodernism seemed to reject the entire mission and purpose of directing. Spectacular transgressions always deserve a closer look.

Prior to the mid-nineteenth century, there were no directors. Instead there were so-called actor-managers who would perform the rudiments of directing, mainly telling the actors where to stand on stage in each scene. But since these actor-managers were usually actors themselves in the production, and leading actors at that, they were equally preoccupied with their own performances. They could not fully commit to being an outside directorial eye. Near the end of the 19th century, there was a push in theatre toward **realism**. This movement, which made its way through all the arts, coincided with advances of the day in industry, science, and medicine. In an important essay on realism, Émile Zola wrote, "There is no reason our art should not portray mankind as precisely and accurately as all other lenses of study." At roughly the same time, in Germany, the opera composer and director, **Richard Wagner**, articulated his theory of the *Gesamtkunstwerk*—a German word meaning, *the complete art work.* Wagner's theory held that all elements of a production—from the text to the acting to the design—should cohere and cooperate with each other. The *Gesamtkunstwerk* theory was, in essence, a call for aesthetic unity in art.

Nowadays we take the idea of unity for granted in theatre or film: if a Tesla drove down the street in a film supposedly set in the 1950s, or if an executive walked into a contemporary office suite wearing an **Elizabethan** doublet and hose, we would immediately spot these anachronisms as being out of place. Before Wagner and Zola, such inconsistencies were commonplace and apparently unremarkable to both artists and audiences. But the call for aesthetic unity necessitated establishing a devoted new staff member in theatre, someone whose job would be to monitor and maintain this unity. This new staff member was the director.

While there is debate over who can rightfully be called the first director, there is generally agreement that by the end of the 19th century, directors had become a fixture in theatre. Over the next half-century, even as theatre explored a variety of styles, from the intense realism of the **Moscow Art Theatre** to the anti-realism of **Bertolt Brecht** to the **absurdism** of **Samuel Beckett**, the role of the director remained consistent as an enforcer of unity. But moving into the second half of the 20th century, in the wake of the unimaginable atrocities of World War II, artists of all kinds began questioning whether the concept of unity still held water. Unity suddenly felt quaint and inadequate for describing the turbulence of the times, and artists started experimenting with disruptions of unity. Postmodernism can be understood in part as an expression of artists' frustrations with the limitations of unity. Postmodernism was a rebellion.

In theatre, postmodernism paved the way for a variety of styles to occupy the stage at once. Suddenly, collage was possible, and the traditional notion of **doing plays in period** was overthrown. For example, a postmodern production of **Medea** might feature one character in a classical Greek robe and another in a contemporary business suit, standing side-by-side, without apology for the incongruity. Postmodernism inspired a wave of collaboration between theatre-makers and artists in other mediums, reinforcing theatre's long history as a multidisciplinary art form. Dance and text were combined so creatively in early postmodern performances that a whole new form, **dance theatre**, emerged—nowhere more rapturously than in the works of **Pina Bausch**. A deluge of hypnotic music, precise movement, and stunning imagery, **Robert Wilson**'s **Einstein on the Beach** challenged ancient assumptions about opera. Productions by **The Wooster Group** blended elements of media and live performance to reflect how technology was influencing people's lives.

Those who opposed postmodernism couched their criticism in the old idea that unity was essential to art. Human beings had an innate preference for unity, these critics contended. We like our clothing and home décor to match. Billions are spent each year making sure major life events—weddings, graduations, holiday parties— are stylish and color-coordinated. Rather than an array of patterns and elements pulling in their own directions, unity ensured consistency and clarity. What troubled these critics most was the threat they felt postmodernism posed to the delicate illusion of realism. **Nora**'s living room in **A Doll's House** is simply more convincing when all the production elements cohere, right? If you made the Christmas tree a palm tree, or had **Torvald** interact with Nora from his study via video chat on a large flat-screen monitor, the integrity of this 19th-century living room would be disturbed, would it not? It would indeed. Directors with a postmodern sensibility would tell you this rupture was exactly what they were after, to reflect a world that had grown infinitely more complex, cacophonous, and diverse than Zola's, Wagner's, or Nora's ever was.

Postmodernism was a celebration of possibility and a rejection of exclusion. While postmodernism is no longer the *ism* of the day, one cannot help but appreciate the extent to which it predicted our present state. Our lives have become postmodern productions. We consume massive amounts of media and information each day, in a variety of different formats, through a dizzying array of platforms, outlets, and sources. We then exchange these ideas with each other across an equally complex network of devices, frequently employing multiple devices at once. Whether we like it or not, our lives have become constant clashes of form and style.

To return to the the main topic of this essay, the Postmodern Choice is a surprise-generating tool inspired by the history and characteristics of postmodernism. Simply put, the Postmodern Choice introduces an element that clashes with the form or style you have previously established in rehearsals. This deliberate disruption instantly precipitates new actions and images in the rehearsal and your directing. If an iPad or a song by Lizzo is inserted into a rehearsal of a period Shakespeare production, new things are bound to happen. To make a Postmodern Choice, ask yourself what does not belong in the world of the play, then courageously interpolate that very thing into the work.

Postmodern Choices may be objects, costumes, bits of text (if you have license to alter the text), gestures, movements, sounds, music, and even fragments of other art works. There is only one rule in making a Postmodern Choice: *be purposeful*. Make Postmodern Choices that illuminate rather than obfuscate. Generating surprise is ultimately a form of experimentation, and the goal of experimentation in theatre should always be to shed greater light on the play, to provide greater access to your audience. The Postmodern Choice should strengthen and not dilute your message, and you should be ready to explain how you are not desecrating the play but enhancing it for our times. Just because the spider has always had eight legs does not mean she cannot these days have nine—and maybe a cowboy boot on the end of the ninth leg for good measure, or a scuba fin, or a tango shoe, or whatever else you can purposefully imagine. You can have fun making a Postmodern Choice, and this sense of enjoyment can revitalize work that feels stale.

The tools described here need not be confined to the rehearsal room or to your work with actors. You can employ these tools in other areas of a production process, for instance in your collaboration with designers. You and the lighting designer might identify a moment where a scene that had been brightly lit can suddenly be plunged into darkness, an application of Do The Opposite (just make sure, for safety, that you give everyone a heads-up before trying this idea). You and the scenic designer might find a moment to drop a bundle of soft feathers on the set's hard concrete floor, or have a field of flowers sprout from it—two design-oriented Left Turns. You and the sound designer could interrupt a track of classical music with thumping techno, and in this moment, the actors could shed their baroque overcoats to reveal cool dance attire beneath—two strong Postmodern Choices.

A compelling production unfurls a chain of well-timed surprises, each arriving just as the power of the last one has worn off. Audiences crave surprise. It is when they do not know where a production is headed, when they cannot predict what will come next, that they are most engaged. You will discover that some performance styles, such as clowning or circus, require surprise more frequently, whereas other styles like realism can get away with deploying surprise more sporadically. Of course, these patterns can always be challenged, which in turn generates more surprise. Between surprises the director must continue making thoughtful choices that justify each moment, each line. Any production that invests only in generating surprise will exhaust its audience. Surprise is the most delicate yet essential ingredient in the dish.

When I was in high school, the greatest thing I ever saw was the musical **Les Misérables**. So many things were great about it, but what I remember loving most were the hope and resolve of the Act I Finale, "One Day More," and Fantine's haunting return from the dead near the end of the show, when she reappears to Jean Valjean as he is about to pass. Then the greatest thing I ever saw was the **SITI Company**'s *War of the Worlds*, directed by **Anne Bogart**, which toured to my university. Specifically it was a moment when the entire ensemble walked together downstage, in perfect synchronicity and slow motion in a shaft of gorgeous light. Then the greatest thing was Brian Dennehey in **Long Day's Journey into Night** on Broadway, and how Dennehy commanded the stage—and my attention—for four hours. What endurance! Then in London, I saw **Caryl Churchill**'s *Far Away,* an object lesson in formal playfulness and experimentation. A prim and proper theatre teacher of mine said disapprovingly, after seeing the production, "Well, I think Ms. Churchill had a little something funny to drink before writing that one!" Delighted, I couldn't agree more. Then a few nights later, I saw Michael Gambon in **Harold Pinter**'s *The Caretaker,* and to this day, it remains the single most convincing performance I have ever seen on stage, transformative beyond the point of transformation, an actor literally *living* as someone else before my very eyes. It was baffling yet exhilarating to learn from Gambon that his main preparation for his first entrance was to sing silly songs backstage and, as he put it, horse around with his mates. Then, I saw The Wooster Group's *To You The Birdie*, a dazzlingly odd adaptation of Jean Racine's *Phèdre* sporting virtuosic badminton-playing and the most precise lighting and sound design I had ever seen in my life—God bless the stage manager of that production! Then I saw **Thomas Ostermeier**'s version of *A Doll's House* at Brooklyn Academy of Music, on tour from the **Schaubühne**, and that was the greatest thing for the way it resuscitated an old play, making it sing again. Then I saw Pina Bausch's *Für die Kinder von gestern, heute und morgen* (For the children of yesterday, today, and tomorrow), and it was overwhelmingly the greatest thing I had ever seen anywhere. I can still feel in my body the experience of watching it, rapt and unable to look away. My concentration intensified feverishly near the end of the performance, around a solo danced by Dominque Mercy. It was so animalistic and graceful at once. It was like lasers shot out from all his limbs, coalescing into a single beam that burned a hole in my heart in the last row of the balcony. Even way up there, this man's movement jostled my molecules, and I understood then what it really means to be moved by art: the impact and effect are corporeal, in the body, in the bones. After this rapture in the theatre, I saw every Pina Bausch piece I could, and her *Vollmond* (Full Moon) became the greatest thing I had ever seen. It rained throughout this piece, creating a veritable lagoon onstage that the performers danced and splashed through! I had never seen such landscape and environment conjured in the theatre. Then I saw **Andrei Şerban**'s ***Uncle Vanya*** in Cluj, Romania. It was a love letter to the theatre and began with an arresting inversion of space. The audience was seated on the stage, and the actors were seated out in the auditorium. As the performance progressed, it repeatedly called attention to the theatre building itself, never allowing me to forget I was in a theatre watching theatre, and I was certain this self-aware production was the greatest thing I had ever seen. But then I saw the six-hour *Sad Face/Happy Face* by **Jan Lauwers** and **Needcompany**, an even more self-aware and metatheatrical performance, with the performers seated onstage in full view the entire time. In the middle of this epic show, during a scene that deals with a couple's grief over a lost child, I found myself wracked with waves of emotion I had never felt before in theatre, or for that matter, in life. Sobs welled up from my guts—spectators near me looked on with concern—and I wondered if this was what the Greeks had meant by **catharsis**. A day later, maybe because I was emotionally sapped, I took great delight in a production directed by **Christoph Marthaler**, where routines of mundane realism were repeatedly interrupted by virtuosic *a cappella* singing! The performers would be sipping tea, then erupt into sacred chorales, then go back to sipping tea. This juxtaposition was so bizarre and amusing that I decided it was the greatest thing I had ever seen—until I saw **Anna Teresa de Keersmaeker**'s *En Atendant*

(Waiting). Beyond the fact that de Keersmaeker's ensemble was dancing site-specifically in a 16th-century cloister to Baroque music played live on antique instruments, which is all pretty lovely to begin with, the production's approach to lighting was revelatory: there wasn't any. The show began at sunset, and after a while, you realized it was becoming quite dark, that no theatrical lighting was being added. The performance plunged further and further into darkness, until you could barely see the performers, and then eventually, you lost them completely—though you could still hear them, the breath of their exertion still echoing off the old stone walls. That was how the performance ended, and all you could conlude was that the dancers and their collective ritual would go on eternally—or at least well beyond the limits of human perception and time. This was, hands down, the most overwhelmingly poetic and profound performance I had ever seen. But then, darn it, I had to admit that **Ariane Mnouchkine**'s *Les Éphémères* (Ephemera)—a sprawling montage of the simple moments of life that change us forever—was even better. Not long after that, I found myself working in Romania on my first international directing gig, experiencing cultural disorientation and homesickness. I saw Andrei Şerban's *Cries and Whispers*, where an actress broke the **fourth wall** and took the hands of a few audience members, mine included, and I felt welcomed and seen in the country for the first time. I knew I would remember this moment forever, marveling at theatre's efficiency in crossing cultural barriers. Then I saw **Angélica Liddell**'s adaptation of Shakespeare's *The Life and Death of King Richard the Third*, a mostly solo performance in which Liddell sustained such an extreme output of energy—an expression of Richard's megalomania—that I had to crown this the greatest thing I had ever seen and Liddell the greatest performer I had ever seen. But wouldn't you know it, on the heels of Liddell's performance, I encountered **Trajal Harrell**'s work for the first time, specifically *Twenty Looks or Paris is Burning at the Judson Church*, and I had to admit Trajal's work was even more powerful because he was not just performing to exhaustion but also running the show at the same time, mixing music live, cleaning and resetting the props, and modifying his fellow performers' choreography in real time before our very eyes. Trajal was performing the act of making a performance, and I could not imagine anything more ambitious until I saw a series of works by Berlin-based **Gob Squad**—*Super Night Shot*, *Are You With Us*, *Help Me Get Through This Night*, and *The Kitchen*. Even more than Trajal, Gob Squad pulled back the curtain on the process of creation, dissected it, writing their own idiosyncratic rules for the show only to then delight in breaking them and writing more. Gob Squad made it hard to tell if they were performing or just being themselves, and I decided this blurry line between art and life was the greatest thing ever and set out to emulate it in my work. But then I saw *Warum läuft Herr R. Amok?* (Why Does Mr. R Run Amok?), directed by the brilliant German director **Susanne**

Kennedy. The actors in Kennedy's production wore stiff plastic masks covering their entire faces. They moved realistically and gestured as if speaking, but they never actually spoke. Instead, their lines were read in over the sound system by other actors who had been placed offstage out of sight. It was like watching a peculiar life-sized puppet show, except the puppets were moving themselves. It felt stiff and inhuman, but since the play was about the vacuousness of 21st-century life, the concept was perfect—a reminder that theatre does not need to be realistic to provide searing social commentary. Yet then I encountered two productions directed by **Milo Rau**, *Hate Radio* and *Five Easy Pieces*. These brave works condemned acts of genocide and abuse, and realism was their driving force. The documentary truth of Rau's productions startled me, and suddenly I wanted nothing more in theatre than real, unmasked human beings sharing true stories. I encountered this even more powerfully in **Back to Back Theatre**'s *The Shadow Whose Prey the Hunter Becomes*, a production that confronted discrimination faced by those living with physical and intellectual disabilities, featuring a cast of actors who all had disabilities themselves. I felt *The Shadow Whose Prey the Hunter Becomes* was the most important performance I had ever seen, for shining a light on a group of individuals we often marginalize and fail to support.

I saw *The Shadow Whose Prey the Hunter Becomes* in early March 2020, right before the Covid-19 pandemic arrived and all the theatres closed. As I write now, this production remains the greatest thing I have ever seen, or perhaps I should say, the *latest* greatest thing I have ever seen. My tendency to revise my tastes could be criticized as an uncertainty about what I really like and am looking for. But I prefer instead to see it as an evolution, a hunger to keep exploring and experiencing a theatrical universe that I recognize is vast beyond my wildest dreams. My list of performances here spans more than twenty years of seeing theatre. I know many of the performances I reference may be obscure to you, and for that, I sincerely apologize. But for once, I believe the obscurity is justified and makes an important point: this is my list and no one else's. Every director needs a list like this that serves as a record of what means most to her in theatre, what she finds most engaging. Identifying the voices and visions you find most captivating is a critical step in clarifying your own artistic agenda. For your list of greatest things to be most effective, it must be deeply personal.

Consuming theatre is part of a director's job, and you should never turn down the chance to see a production, provided you have the resources to do so. Your directorial vocabulary will expand mainly by seeing or studying the work of other directors. We develop our own style and aesthetics through a process of absorbing others' ideas, digesting and reflecting upon them, and then transforming them into something new*ish* that serves our needs.

Do not waste your time trying to be original. Originality happens rarely and usually by accident, so it is not really a constructive goal to set for yourself. Instead of invention, think about recycling and rearrangement, starting from something you already know. For example, rather than saying, "How can I direct *The Seagull* in a completely new way," ask yourself, "How would Pina Bausch direct *The Seagull*?" Since Pina Bausch never directed *The Seagull*, there is novelty in this idea. Consider for instance Bausch's *Der Fensterputzer* (The Window Washer), dominated by an enormous pile of flower petals. Flower petals don't feel quite right for *The Seagull*, but wouldn't it be fantastic for a production to feature an enormous pile of feathers? I landed on this fresh idea not by staring at the wall, wracking my brain for an original way of directing *The Seagull*, but by simply looking at the play through the lens of an artist I admire.

As you absorb the work of other directors and artists, keep your eyes and heart open. Bear in mind that our first response to art is usually emotional. Push beyond *like* to *intent*. The casual spectator can get away with merely liking or not liking things, but that is only superficial engagement. You should tunnel deeper into the work, identifying what the artist's intentions and methods were and assessing whether she achieved them. Will yourself to remember everything you can, the good and the bad. Do not go to the theatre without a small journal in your pocket to jot down notes after everything you see, especially after seeing something great. These notes will become a reservoir of inspiration to which you can repeatedly return. Although I mainly confined my list here to theatre, you should seek out, and let yourself be wowed by, great art of all kinds. When you are at a creative impasse and don't know what to do, the best remedy is often to seek inspiration from art in other mediums. Go to a museum, or a film, or a concert, or a poetry slam, or a cooking class. Briefly immersing yourself in alternative creative ideas can dislodge whatever has been gumming up your works, restoring your flow.

As I write this, I recognize that seeing theatre has become a privilege. And unfortunately, while digital theatre has increased accessibility and lowered the price of admission, it is not a replacement for live theatre. Theatre is an immersive and collective experience brought into focus by watching and breathing with others around you—including the performers. The Covid-19 pandemic highlighted how fundamental shared space is to the theatrical experience. In May and June of 2020, in the early months of the pandemic, I set out to create an online production. With my collaborators I planned to create "a straightforward and fun play about a Zoom dinner party"—my words to the company as we began rehearsals. Eight weeks later, after too many creative fits and starts to count, our project had been retitled, *Inconceivable*, and it had become a meditation on the impossibility of making theatre when we are not physically together. A Zoom room is not a real room. Theatre's survival rests upon its continued commitment to shared space and to delivering its ideas in-person, so long as it is safe to do so. Sadly, we now recognize that anything delivered digitally can be manipulated and distorted. But the reality of an actor standing and speaking a few feet away from you is never in dispute, and the pain, joy, or even outrage this engenders in you will always be genuine. You cannot deep fake performance in shared space. Theatre, it turns out, may be a salvation in times where we struggle to agree upon the truth. Theatre has the capacity to set the record straight, and in doing so, to heal us. Through theatre, we can learn to trust each other again.

A director cannot appreciate the power of shared space, and then learn to create and sustain it in his own performances, without first experiencing it many times himself as a spectator. All with power and influence must push tirelessly to increase theatre students' access to live performances. Students should hold their teachers, mentors, and institutions of study accountable for this, and they should feel empowered to speak up when theatre around them seems too scarce. Keep in mind that great work is happening everywhere, and certainly not just in the mainstream or on Broadway, where rising ticket prices continue creating barriers for many to attend. Great theatre and directing is happening in regional theatres and community theatres; in found spaces, store fronts, and art galleries; even outdoors and in the street. Go find transcendent work off the beaten path and support the artists making it.

And one more thing: whittle down your list of greatest things to a handful of absolute favorites—perhaps three or four productions. These will be your lifelines, and you will keep them in your back pocket, so to speak, to call upon if all else fails, or in the event you ever need a reminder of the power and beauty of theatre—its potential on its best days to change our lives and maybe even the world.

1. Our theatre will address our community.

2. Our theatre will include our community.

3. We will consider our community to be all those around us who we already know, as well as those around us who we don't yet know but should. This means our community will always be growing.

4. We will work in a clear and direct way to ensure our audiences always understand our productions, even if they are newcomers to theatre.

5. Accessibility will become a permanent priority and consideration in our work, as central to the production as its script, scenery, or casting. Directing a production that excludes audience on any grounds—physical, intellectual, financial, or otherwise—will be counted as a directorial failure. Accessibility has been understood to mean opening doors, but now it should include resources for stepping through those doors, too, and making sense of what's inside. Simply giving someone a free ticket is no longer enough.

6. We will all be teachers, even if we are still learning ourselves, and we will understand teaching as central to our directing.

7. We will make every effort to work with local actors from our community. Theatre for our community must be made with our community.

8. We will set realism aside as an aesthetic and tool. For the moment, **Henrik Ibsen** has outstayed his welcome. Our audiences aren't homogenous enough anymore, thank goodness, to sustain realism. A single sculpted illusion in the proscenium arch will never hold their collective attention. Instead, our productions will tear down the proscenium to offer a buffet of potential realities to satisfy the spectacular diversity of identities and interests comprising our new audiences.

9. We will lay to rest the stereotype of the director—or any artist—as an aloof genius, dolling out brilliance at his parsimonious discretion. Auteur moodiness has no place in a theatre of engagement.

10. How we talk about our work will be as important as the work itself. If we cannot explain a scene or gesture we will cut it from the production. Art should indeed be a place to investigate the nonliteral, the expressive. It should be a place to see what we can say without words, or by rearranging words in new ways, and these forays into new language may challenge the spectator. But we must always be able to explain our intentions. Our work can be abstract, but our explanations of it should never be. Over the years some directors have taken strange pleasure in baffling audiences, as if inscrutability were

a mark of artistic quality. It is not. Creating confusion is quite easy. Telling a story with clarity and purpose is far harder, and as such, a nobler pursuit.

11. The production will no longer be the conclusion and apotheosis of the rehearsal process. Rather, it will be a catalyst for the dialogue and engagement that will follow the production.

12. The practice of the director leaving the production immediately after its premiere will end, and he will remain in town to facilitate this dialogue and engagement. In professional settings, directors' contracts will be extended to enable this. This engagement, which will aim to produce measurable community impact, will be treated with as much care and respect as the production itself.

13. Every production will offer audience members the chance to donate to a cause of great relevance in the community. Donations will not be only monetary. Directors will collaborate with the producers and artistic leaders of the theatre to determine the cause that will be supported.

14. Every academic department will appoint a theatre practitioner to its faculty. Theatre will become a megaphone for promoting and explaining groundbreaking research that might otherwise remain

inaccessible or impenetrable to the general public.

15. We will make every effort to stage our productions outside traditional theatre venues, and when we do, we will no longer employ the label *site-specific* to describe these performances. This label applies an unhelpful asterisk, creating the impression that theatre in nontraditional settings must be justified, announced, excused. In reality, all theatre is specific to its site. If it is staged in a traditional theatre, it is specific to that building and architecture, and if it is staged in the street or on a beach or in a gymnasium, it responds to those settings. Going forward, we will call everything theatre, regardless of where it is staged. We will regard the church, the public school, the hospital cafeteria, the assisted living facility, as primary stages, uniquely suited to provide direct encounters with our community. Staging a play in a preschool or community center will be as important to us, personally and professionally, as directing on a major regional or national stage. We will accept this means rehearsing in conditions that may be different from those we are accustomed to in traditional venues.

16. We will not fetishize community by exporting local stories to national stages. A play about a group of veterans will be staged at a VA hospital. A play about the opioid crisis will be staged in a treatment center. A play about the impact of the waning coal industry on rural communities will be staged in community theatres in southeastern Ohio and northern West Virginia and western Pennsylvania rather than New York City. A play about a lack of childcare will be staged for an audience of parents in a living room, and perhaps the parents will even participate in the performance.

17. We will value our community's opinion of our work above our own. The director has frequently been described as a production's first spectator, but we will reckon with the flaw in that idea. The director has never been a good proxy for the audience. Whereas the director has seen the production develop every day, over a period of weeks if not months, members of the audience will see the production just once, like a train rushing by. They will never be able to appreciate the director's work at the same level of granular detail that the director herself can. We directors all too often lose track of what is really detectable in a play upon a first (and only) encounter. For this reason, audience feedback has always been valuable for directors, and as we increasingly engage our community, it will be even more essential to hear and heed their response. We will invite feedback from our community from the earliest moments of the rehearsal process. Chairs will always be set out in our rehearsal rooms for community members. We will radically overturn the notion of the rehearsal process as a secret ritual with restricted access.

18. Productions will be staged with the utter conviction that they are happening here and now. Every production will find a way to exclaim, "We are here!"

19. We will end the practice of doing plays in period. We will still direct Chekhov, Shakespeare, and other old plays, but we will always set them in a contemporary context. If directors and designers want to use old costumes and objects, they will mix and match eras and styles, resisting historical fidelity. For instance, a character in an Elizabethan gown might wear Converse sneakers, or Shakespeare's Hamlet might sport a pair of aviators, masking his grief. Setting films in a historical period may not dull their capacity to engage, but theatre is different. Theatre unfolds live in the same space with its audience. There is no screen separating audience from art. Breathing the same air as the performers, the audience is compelled to acknowledge and enter the world we put on stage because we're all in the same room together. With so much for us to discuss and work out in the world right now, why flee to the past—and drag our audience with us? If directors and designers cannot resist the temptation of setting a play in period, they should discard the play and direct something else.

20. We will consider how major social and political issues impacting our community—such as access to clean water or affordable housing—might be addressed with theatre, offering up theatre not just as an art but also as a tool. We will concern ourselves less with *what theatre is*, a well-worn topic by now, and more with *what theatre can do*.

21. Engaging will not mean abandoning or compromising our creative ambitions. On the contrary, we will demonstrate that socially engaged, community-centered work can be just as slick and professional as a Broadway production. For example, we will create a captivating piece of **immersive theatre**—like *Sleep No More* by **Punchdrunk**—that explores climate change. We will confront racial injustice and the need for reformed policing in a new musical with an irresistible soundtrack you can't stop humming.

22. Theatres demonstrating measurable community impact will receive government grants and subsidies, incentivizing them to continue engaging their communities while reducing their reliance on private funding streams.

23. We will regard theatre as public service and ourselves as public servants.

24. We will recognize that engaging effectively with others first and foremost requires engaging with ourselves. We will be honest about who we are and what we can do. There has recently been a wellspring of important conversation around dissolving ancient, stubborn hierarchies of power in workplaces and redistributing that power more broadly and equitably. It is concerning that directors have often possessed disproportionate power and control compared to others. This imbalance is even more alarming when we consider that the field of directing has historically been dominated by a single group—white men. This means that since the advent of the director more than a century ago, the vast majority of theatre rehearsal rooms have exhibited and perpetuated white male supremacy. This is shameful and obviously obstructive to engagement: if theatre continues to be led overwhelmingly by the same kind of people, how can it ever extend its reach, attract new audiences, or appeal to those community members who feel left out? In communities where the same people have been directing over and over again, one dramatic solution would be to eliminate the office of the director altogether, or at least severely limit his power, redistributing it back to the actors and the rest of the creative team. But eliminating the director risks resurrecting old problems theatre sought to solve with the invention of the director in the first place. The director's capacity to shape and monitor the production from the outside is worth preserving, especially with increased attention being paid to matters of representation and messaging. A better solution for decentralizing directorial power would be to explore models of collective directing whereby the lone director is replaced by a committee of two or more directorial presences, each given roughly the same amount of responsibility. Collective directing is not a new idea, but it has never caught on in theatre. The most common objections to collective directing are, not surprisingly, that the committee of directors never manages to negotiate an equitable power-sharing arrangement, or that their collective creativity fails to congeal into a clear approach that their collaborators can act upon. But these are not fatal flaws, and they can be overcome. **Devised theatre** and other models of ensemble creation offer wisdom and practical advice for sharing and sorting out leadership between two or more individuals. Going forward, collective directing models deserve greater attention. It would be beneficial for directing courses and programs currently advancing only the lone director model to assign their students projects requiring collective directing as well. We will see more collective directing in the future. We are already seeing collectivity in artistic leadership, with major American theatres like the Wilma in Philadelphia and Steppenwolf in Chicago electing to distribute the **artistic director** role among more than one individual. For the moment, there is a simple way of dealing with groups who have been disproportionately empowered as directors: we stop giving them work. We stop today, and we stop now. We do not need to eliminate an office in the theatre that has done, and can continue to do, measurable good, but we desperately need to change who occupies that office. Rather than eliminating the power centered around the position of the director, we will reallocate it. The director's power can be reparative when put in the hands of those individuals— mainly people of color and women—who have been historically underrepresented in our field. I challenge all of us who have been privileged, recognized, awarded, appointed, supported, or simply seen, to take the time and energy we would ordinarily spend furthering our own careers and to invest these resources instead in advancing the careers of directors who our profession has not yet supported or seen. The role of the historically overrepresented director right now is not to direct theatre; it is to park himself on the sidelines and cheer others on. But this effort cannot fall exclusively to directors. It must also be taken up by artistic directors and producers who do the hiring and staffing within theatre organizations. As preparers of the next generation of theatre artists, theatre educators and directing training programs must champion this movement, too. Curricular revision to embrace more diverse perspectives and anti-racist pedagogies is essential, but it will take us only so far. We need to physically effect and manifest diversity. We need unsung voices, untold stories, and overlooked identities in our classrooms, on our stages, right now. Recruitment of underrepresented students will become an institutional priority, taken up by devoted experts with passion and vision. Institutions will reallocate sizable portions of their development budgets to recruiting such individuals because this is far more important than throwing another gala or erecting another building. Universities will set aggressive recruiting goals and suspend the operations of programs that fail to meet them. We will hold our employers, our teachers, our institutions, and most of all, ourselves, to radical account on these matters.

25. We will be kind at every turn.

Film is a photographic medium capturing and framing worlds that already exist. Theatre, on the other hand, creates worlds through collaboration with our imaginations. In a film, if a character says, "Here is a garden," the viewer expects to see a real garden on the screen, and the film is obligated to provide one. Inside a theatre, however, where the viewer accepts a real garden cannot exist, there is more flexibility in representing the garden. The garden may be depicted in great detail with lots of scenery or more minimally with just a few items, in this case perhaps a mound of dirt and a few artificial plants. It is even acceptable in theatre for the production to provide no scenery at all—for the stage to be empty, leaving the audience to conjure the garden entirely in their minds. For the vast majority of its history, this is exactly how theatre has been presented: on empty stages and bare platforms bearing no resemblance whatsoever to the environments described in the text of the play.

Theatre has always expected the audience to do some work to see, and to believe, what is being described on the stage (this idea is famously explored in Peter Brook's **The Empty Space**). The audience's willingness to play along and indulge their imaginations enables a very useful process I call *conversion*. The way it works is simple. Any object that seems to be one thing can become another thing in the minds of the audience, as long as the actors and the play itself sufficiently adopt and support the change. A nondescript wooden box, not unlike those you encounter in many rehearsal rooms, might serve within the same production as a chair, bed, tree trunk, and treasure chest.

Conversions may occur anytime, even in the middle of a scene. For instance, an actor playing a king may be sitting on a chair that we understand to be his throne. But if, later in the scene, another character declares, "Here is the king sitting on the commode!" and if the text and actors suddenly adjust to support this abrupt conversion, then the audience will very quickly accept the chair as a toilet, too. While theatre always demands real action, it does not require realistic scenery or design. Before investing in costly, realistic production elements, directors and designers should consider whether conversion and the power of the imagination might fill the stage just as well. There are so many benefits to doing so. Working with less saves money, reduces waste, and is more environmentally sustainable. It enables swift transitions between scenes that reduce technical complexity and thus the possibility that something could go wrong. Quick transitions also allow exciting contrasts to emerge. In the example above, cutting quickly from a king on a throne to a king on the commode may speak to the blurring of public and private spaces in a play or the indecorous behavior of politicians. In its first few minutes, Richard Loncraine's film version of Shakespeare's *The Life and Death of King Richard the Third* essentially executes this same cut. But since it is a film, the two scenes are staged in two different locations, a grand banquet hall and the bathroom. Theatre on the other hand can transport us from one location to another in the blink of an eye, without the slightest physical adjustment on stage—though a strong change of lighting or sound may help. Finally, working with less stimulates the audience more than handing them everything on a plate. It strengthens their engagement. When an actor stands on a bare stage and says, "Here is a garden," the audience must sit forward and look for it; when an actor says the same while surrounded by an exquisitely realistic scenic design, or while standing in a real garden in a film, the audience is not obligated to search. While they may appreciate the image handed to them, they are not invited to contribute to its creation. Their participation has been discouraged.

Working with less is one thread of a larger creative principal I describe as *working with what you have*. If there is one idea you take away from this book, I hope it will be this. It is the best creative catalyst I know, the best way of treating your directing with the care and grace it deserves. *Working with what you have* means you always have enough.

Working with what you have means your senses are wide open like never before, and your heart is, too. *Working with what you have* means you can start directing now, today, rather than tomorrow or when the producer gets around to giving you the green light. *Working with what you have* means you can stretch $50 as far as $500. It is a frugal, resourceful, and admired approach across the field. It is practical, not aspirational or abstract, and gritty, inventive, and even a little sly. Without unnecessary objects to distract you, your attention comes back, keen and sharp, to exactly what is before you—the space, your team, and the play. You may find yourself falling in love with the play all over again. You start thinking of space less as a container and more as a collaborator, and you become hungry for opportunities to work in nontraditional spaces whose idiosyncrasies you can celebrate. *Working with what you have* results in work that is more accessible because the work has been made with gratitude for what you have rather than bitterness for what you lack, and gratitude in a performance is never lost on an audience.

Working with what you have means you are always enough, and you don't need to lament or feel embarrassed about what you don't have, because there is nothing else you need. Even nothing will be sufficient. In fact, nothing will be plenty. And *you* will be plenty, and the time and place you are standing in, right here, right now, is perfect.

Except what if it isn't?

What if the place you are in is decidedly not perfect or doesn't feel anywhere close to right? What if everything about it actually feels wrong?

What if you do feel embarrassed about what you are missing? What if your lament is loud and real and long? What if your heart is heavy? What if you are in pain or grief? What if you are contending with a mental health disorder? What if you are caring for a friend or a family member who is sick, so that most of your love goes to them, and there is precious little left for you? What if you are stigmatized, marginalized, vulnerable, or unheard and unseen? What if you cannot find shelter? What if you are displaced? What if your access to water and medicine is in peril? What if police and doctors frighten you? What if you have no family, or have lost the family you had?

I hope none of this describes you, but I also know it might. The world has not been calm or easy lately. Here are some things that have happened in just the last few years. Be advised that what follows may be difficult to read.

President Donald Trump was impeached (for the first time) on the charge of abusing his power of office and eventually acquitted by a Republican-controlled Congress. The Covid-19 pandemic emerged and ravaged the world, causing disruption and loss for virtually every citizen on the planet, though vulnerable and marginalized populations were disproportionately affected. Unemployment rates skyrocketed to 14.7 percent in the United States. Ahmaud Arbery, an unarmed Black man, was shot and killed by two white men while jogging in Georgia. Breonna Taylor, an unarmed Black woman, was shot and killed in her home in Louisville, Kentucky by police. In Minneapolis, Minnesota, police officer Derek Chauvin pressed his knee into the neck of George Floyd, an unarmed Black man, for more than eight minutes, killing Floyd and sparking worldwide protests for racial justice. In Beirut 170 people were killed in an explosion of improperly stored chemicals. The largest and most destructive wildfires in California's history scorched more than two million acres. Feminist and women's rights advocate, Ruth Bader-Ginsburg, died of cancer, vacating her seat on the Supreme Court. Also, John Lewis, the Reverend Joseph E. Lowery, Desmond Tutu, and Earl Old Person died. Chick Corea, John Prine, and Stephen Sondheim died. The amazing actors Chadwick Bosemann, Rebecca Luker, and Nick Cordero—all too young—died. Tony Hsieh died. Larry Kramer died. Joan Didion died. Ming Cho Lee died. Anna Halprin died. Joe Morgan died. Even Alex Trebek died. The US Capitol building was stormed by a violent mob seeking to disrupt the certification of electoral votes from the 2020 US Presidential Election. Accused of inciting the mob, President Donald Trump became the only US president to be impeached a second time. Winter storms devastated Texas and its power supply, killing more than 200 in one of the state's worst weather-related disasters. Daunte Wright, an unarmed Black man, was shot during a routine traffic stop by police officer Kim Potter, who claimed she meant to fire a taser rather than a firearm. A beachside condominium in Miami collapsed, killing ninety-eight people. Following a chaotic withdrawal of the US military from

Afghanistan, the Taliban overthrew the Afghan government and retook control of the country. Hurricane Ida, the most devastating storm to hit the Southeast coast of the United States since Hurricane Katrina in 2005, claimed the lives of nearly 100 across six states. Tornadoes ripped through Kentucky just before Christmas 2021, killing seventy-nine and leaving thousands without shelter for the holidays. Inflation reached its highest levels since the 1980s, sparking global economic concern and fears of recession. Rates of depression and anxiety soared, particularly among young adults. US Surgeon General Vivek Murthy declared loneliness a public health crisis. Drug overdoses skyrocketed, driven by a surge of the synthetic opioid, fentanyl, in the drug market. Russia began a military assault on Ukraine, killing thousands, leveling cities, and triggering the largest refugee crisis in Europe since World War II. The Supreme Court of the United States eliminated the constitutional right to obtain an abortion.

If any of these calamities has touched you in some way, and statistically there's a good chance one of them has, I'm deeply sorry for what you have experienced. You may not want to work with what you have because you may be standing in a place of pain or fear. You may want nothing more than to escape what you have and where you are. If you have the means and opportunity to relocate yourself to a place that feels safer, more comfortable, more healthy, more open, you should do so. Go right now.

But what if you can't? What if you lack the financial resources to leave? What if your immune system is compromised? What if you don't have enough food or fuel for the journey? Relocation is a privilege not available to everyone. You may find yourself with no choice but to work with what you have, and even as you come to terms with this, you may find yourself doubting whether theatre makes any sense. Given your disappointment and discomfort, how can it possibly be a time for theatricality and play? Isn't the imaginary landscape of theatre vulgar next to what is happening in our marginalized communities, in our courtrooms, in our forests, in Ukraine? How can we sing, dance, and speak in pretty monologues when many among us aren't even allowed to express their most basic human needs? How can we even conceive of theatre in this time, in this place?

Maybe only as a dream, a wild and hopeful dream. A dream in which we give ourselves the chance to reboot, repair, rebuild the world as we would have it. That's the only way I see theatre making sense in hard times. In laughter, fury, tears, or whatever expression feels right, theatre imagines a better place, a place where we can heal.

The theatre in my dreams is a theatre of solutions, purpose, and possibility. A theatre not confined to realism because everyone's reality is different. A theatre that looks forward not backward. A theatre full of singing and dancing, not just among the performers but the audience too, if they are willing. I want theatre to include everyone—the show is always better that way.

The theatre in my dreams shines a bright light on the shadowy places desperate to be seen. It not only believes in change but effects it. It cherishes people's time and never wastes it. It's a theatre in love with stories, the stories I love and weep for, and I share my tears openly with my colleagues. It's a theatre that is committed and devoted, that redeems, transcends, and forgives. It's a theatre that makes us whole again.

Despite all our missteps, our failures, our inequities, disparities, oversights, our clumsiness, our coarseness, our wastefulness, our judgment, our lack of compassion when it was needed most, our petty disputes, our wildfires, our pandemics, our wars—despite all the times we should have been better and kinder than we were, the theatre in my dreams still, somehow, believes in us. And of course, it still believes in theatre.

We are moving forward. A seismic shift is underway. The old titans are falling, crumbling in their inflexibility, and sweeping into the vacuum their departure shall leave, before the dust has even settled, will be you. You and your dreams are the future. We believe in you more than you know, and your work is unspeakably gorgeous. You can do this. So go, direct your heart out.

Exercises

Here are suggestions for quickly putting each essay into practice in a classroom or rehearsal setting. I hope these ideas might inspire you to design your own exercises and applications:

1

Make a list of things that excite you, that you really care about, that might even make you cry. Don't strain to make these things theatre-related (although if some of them are, that's fine). When you feel like you're done with your list, stop and look it over. Rearrange your list with the items you care more about at the top and those you care less about at the bottom. Sit back and contemplate your list, especially the items at the top. What do you feel in your body as you envision these things? What goes through your mind, and through your heart?

2

Consider the opening scene of *The Seagull* (Appendix 2). Plan a detailed sequence of actions, at least two minutes in duration, that can precede and motivate Medvedenko's first line. Stage this sequence with two actors and adjust until all three of you are satisfied. Then collaborate together to create another sequence of actions that is wildly different from the first sequence but just as effective in motivating Medvedenko's first line. Stage and try out this second option, and keep whichever sequence you like best.

3

Instead of doing table work at a table, do it in a circle of chairs, or seated on mats on the floor. Removing the table encourages more doing and less talking by making everyone immediately feel like they're occupying a stage, a world, together. You don't need a table to do table work.

4

Freeze a scene at any point during rehearsal, preferably when you have several actors on stage, and ask each actor to tell you what their character wants in the scene (their objective), how they are trying to accomplish it (their action), and what stands in their way (their obstacle). An actor should be able to answer each of these questions quickly and clearly in a single sentence—and a director should be able to as well. But be patient: it may take time to achieve this precision. Use this exercise sparingly, no more than once or twice in a rehearsal.

5

Think about your basic habits as a director. If you usually sit in rehearsals, try standing. If you usually work with the studio blinds drawn and the fluorescent lights buzzing overhead, try opening the blinds and working with natural light. If you usually break the day up into two sessions with one long break in the middle, try breaking the day up into three sessions with two short breaks. If the rehearsal room is always quiet when the actors arrive, try having some music playing in the background to enliven the space. In other words, choose an aspect of your directing that has become routine and deliberately disrupt it. How does this adjustment affect you, others, and the process as a whole?

6

Take a two-character scene that has already been staged. Explain the concept of Do the Opposite to the actors. Tell them they are each free, anywhere they wish in the scene, to Do the Opposite. Underline the importance of safety and how their choice must not put themselves or anyone else in the room, including their scene partner, at risk. Run the scene. The exercise can also be done with the director, rather than the actors, determining where to Do the Opposite. Or, if you really want to have fun, actors and directors can both be allowed to use the tool. Whichever variation you use, make sure you come together at the end to discuss the new material that was stirred up, so that it can be preserved if you wish. It may also be helpful to set a limit on the number of times the tool can be used in a single rehearsal of a scene—three times would be reasonable. If the tool is overused, its effectiveness may be diminished.

7

What is the absolute best piece of art or entertainment you have seen recently? Why did you like it so much? And what was the best piece you saw before that and why did you like that one so much? And before that? Write your responses on the first page of a new notebook or journal. . . .

8

First, answer this question: who do you think of as your community? Then, answer this: what could you add to your work right now, right this very moment, to make your directing more inclusive of, and accessible to, that community? What you add doesn't need to be grand or complex. It just needs to be sensitive and intentional. Implement the change in your next rehearsal.

9

This exercise deals with conversion of a prop. Find an object already in the room. It may be yours, or it may be a colleague's (please ask their permission to use it!). It should be a real object, like a hairbrush, hat, umbrella, or birdcage—it's always fun to work with an unusual object. Stage an actor in *expected relationship* to the object—that is, doing the thing one would be expected to do with the object. For example, if the object is a hairbrush, you would first stage the actor combing his hair. Then convert the object twice into two new objects by creating two new relationships between your actor and the object. For instance, you might convert the brush into a phone by having the actor bring the brush to his ear. Then you might convert the brush into a flashlight by having the actor hold it out in front of himself, crouch down, and slowly advance forward, as if moving through a dark tunnel. Make sure to address the transitions between the conversions as well. How can the actor move creatively from brushing his hair to talking on the phone to exploring a tunnel? Doing this exercise without text (or with very limited text) will amplify the physicality of the conversions.

Appendix 2

Opening Scene of The Seagull *by Anton Chekhov, translated by Marian Feld*

The scene is laid in the park on Sorin's estate. A broad avenue of trees leads away from the audience toward a lake which lies lost in the depths of the park. The avenue is obstructed by a rough stage, temporarily erected for the performance of amateur theatricals, and which screens the lake from view. There is a dense growth of bushes to the left and right of the stage. A few chairs and a little table are placed in front of the stage. The sun has just set. Masha and Medvedenko enter.

Medvedenko Why do you always wear mourning?

Masha I dress in black to match my life. I am unhappy.

Medvedenko Why should you be unhappy? I don't understand it. You are healthy, and though your father is not rich, he has a good competency. My life is far harder than yours. I only have twenty-three roubles a month to live on, but I don't wear mourning.

Masha Happiness does not depend on riches; poor men are often happy.

Medvedenko In theory, yes, but not in reality. Take my case, for instance; my mother, my two sisters, my little brother and I must all live somehow on my salary of twenty-three roubles a month. We have to eat and drink, I take it. You wouldn't have us go without tea and sugar, would you? Or tobacco? Answer me that, if you can.

Masha The play will soon begin.

Medvedenko Yes, Nina Zarechnaya is going to act in Konstantin's play. They love one another, and their two souls will unite tonight in the effort to interpret the same idea by different means. There is no ground on which your soul and mine can meet. I love you. Too restless and sad to stay at home, I tramp here every day, six miles and back, to be met only by your indifference. I am poor, my family is large, you can have no inducement to marry a man who cannot even find sufficient food for his own mouth.

Masha It is not that. *(She takes snuff)* I am touched by your affection, but I cannot return it, that is all. *(She offers him the snuff-box)* Will you take some?

Medvedenko No, thank you.

Masha The air is sultry; a storm is brewing for tonight. You do nothing but moralize or else talk about money. To you, poverty is the greatest misfortune that can befall a man, but I think it is a thousand times easier to go begging in rags than to—You wouldn't understand that, though.

Glossary

A Doll's House Henrik Ibsen's landmark play, premiered in 1879, that signaled the dawn of realism.

A Streetcar Named Desire Tennessee Williams's 1947 play about toxic masculinity and our willingness to empathize with the lost and broken among us. Features the famous characters of Blanche DuBois and Stanley Kowalski.

Absurdism Emerging in the wake of World War II, a theatrical style that represented life as chaotic and illogical. Associated with the works of Eugène Ionesco and Samuel Beckett.

Action A character's tactic for pursuing his objective.

Andrei Şerban Romanian director known for staging classical plays in a nonrealistic style that plainly acknowledges the artifice of theatre.

Angélica Liddell Spanish writer, director, and actor known for making physically demanding performances.

Anna Teresa de Keersmaeker Contemporary Belgian choreographer whose work is known for minimalism, repetition, and close coordination with musicians.

Anne Bogart American director and founder of the SITI Company who developed Viewpoints, a system of ensemble creation and kinesthetic awareness.

Anton Chekhov Russian author of *The Seagull* and other plays prized for their detailed characterization and emotional depth. Closely associated with Konstantin Stanislavski, who directed the premieres of most of Chekhov's major plays.

Ariane Mnouchkine French director and founder of *Théâtre du Soleil* (Theatre of the Sun), a company known for its ensemble-driven productions that often explore international performance styles.

Artistic Director The leader and chief executive of a theatre organization.

Back to Back Theatre Australian theatre company invested in challenging stereotypes connected to ableism and disability.

Bertolt Brecht German playwright and director who criticized realism for lulling the spectator into a passive viewing experience. Brecht felt a performance must deliberately disrupt realism—for instance by having a character burst into song or suddenly address the audience—in order to invite the deepest reflection and engagement from its audience.

Caryl Churchill British playwright renown for her formal daring and examination of feminism, politics, and power.

Catharsis A release and purge of emotions in response to witnessing theatre, first theorized by the Ancient Greek philosopher Aristotle.

Christoph Marthaler Swiss director whose performances combine elements of realism, clowning, and exquisite musicality.

Dance Theatre A form of performance that blends movement, spoken text, and dramatic situation, epitomized by the work of Pina Bausch.

Death of a Salesman Arthur Miller's tragedy of 1948 where Willy Loman grapples with the dissolution of his career, dreams, and family.

Devised theatre An original performance created from scratch, often by a team of artists working collaboratively.

Doing plays in period Taking great care in every aspect of a production to establish and maintain an illusion of a prior era. When a classical play is done in period, it usually means the production is set at the time the play was originally written.

Einstein on the Beach Directed by Robert Wilson and premiered in 1976, a groundbreaking opera that blended contemporary dance, a hypnotic score by Philip Glass, and stunning visuals into a non-narrative structure that was highly unusual in opera at the time.

Elizabeth LeCompte American director and cofounder of The Wooster Group. LeCompte has directed nearly all of The Wooster Group's productions since its founding in 1975.

Elizabethan Referring to the reign of Queen Elizabeth I in England, an era when theatre flourished and Shakespeare wrote his plays.

Fight choreography Careful staging of physical violence in the play that creates a convincing illusion while always prioritizing performers' safety. Conducted by a Fight Choreographer.

Fourth wall An imaginary barrier between the performers and the audience. When we speak of the fourth wall being up or maintained, the actors do not acknowledge the audience. Conversely, when we say the fourth wall has been broken or is down, actors may address or engage with the audience, sometimes even performing among them.

Gob Squad Award-winning Berlin-based theatre company that playfully blurs the line between offstage and onstage, actor and character, often through the use of video and other media.

Harold Pinter Prolific British playwright famous for tense, terse plays exploring power and manipulation.

Henrik Ibsen Norwegian playwright and author of *A Doll's House*. Credited with initiating a trend in playwriting toward realism.

Immersive theatre A performance where the fourth wall is usually down and the performers and audience mingle freely in the same space. The performance surrounds, or immerses, the audience.

Intimacy direction The staging of all moments of a play dealing with intimate contact or sexual situations. Conducted by an Intimacy Director who brings special expertise in guiding actors to the safe and authentic representation of this material on stage.

Jan Lauwers Belgian director known for making multidisciplinary theatre performances that combine text, music, dance, and visual art. Trained as a painter, Lauwers describes the stage as a canvas.

Joanne Akalaitis Lithuanian American theatre director.

Joseph Chaikin American actor and director who founded the Open Theatre, one of the first physical theatre ensembles in the United States.

Judith Malina American actor, director, and cofounder of the Living Theatre, a company that rose to prominence in the 1950s and that was inspired by Bertolt Brecht's ideas about anti-realism and audience engagement.

Julian Beck American actor, director, and cofounder of the Living Theatre along with Judith Malina.

Konstantin Stanislavski Russian actor, director, teacher, and theorist who pioneered a system for achieving physical and emotional authenticity in acting. Most modern acting techniques descend from Stanislavski's ideas.

Lee Breuer American playwright, director, and founding member of Mabou Mines, an influential experimental theatre company in New York.

Les Misérables Musical by Claude-Michel Schönberg and Alain Boublil, based on the novel by Victor Hugo.

Long Day's Journey into Night Eugene O'Neill's best-known play about failure, addiction, and strained family relationships.

Macbeth Title character in Shakespeare's play *The Tragedy of Macbeth*, who murders to secure and maintain power.

Medea Ancient Greek tragedy by Euripides.

Milo Rau Swiss director known for documentary-based, politically engaged performances.

Moscow Art Theatre Founded in Moscow in 1898 by Konstantin Stanislavski and closely associated with Stanislavski's system of acting, which Stanislavski developed in a series of productions at the theatre. Most of Anton Chekhov's major plays premiered at the Moscow Art Theatre under Stanislavski's direction.

Needcompany Belgian dance theatre ensemble.

Nora Protagonist of *A Doll's House* and one of modern drama's most famous characters who places herself and her own needs ahead of her husband's—a radical and transgressive act for audiences in 1879, when the play premiered.

Objective What a character wants to accomplish in a scene, the character's goal.

Peter Brook British director who established a multinational ensemble dedicated to investigating the fundamental ingredients of theatre and the performer-spectator encounter. Known for actor-driven productions with very little scenery, an approach he explained in his book, *The Empty Space*.

Pina Bausch German dance theatre artist who, together with her company, Tanztheater Wuppertal, created works of deep humanity and astonishing beauty that often featured her dancers engaging with natural materials—soil, water, tree branches, grass, and memorably, a field of carnations. But silliness and whimsicality permeated her work, too, like the hippopotamus that turned up in one piece and the alligator in another (these were both puppets of course). The fourth wall was always fluid in her performances: a dancer might interrupt an exquisite movement sequence to pick up a microphone and speak directly to the audience, then go right back to moving again. And always, Bausch's choice of musical accompaniment seemed perfect. Though she died, in 2010, Tanztheater Wuppertal continues performing her works, nourishing her legacy.

Punchdrunk British theatre company known for their immersive performances.

Realism Style of theatre that aims to represent people, objects, and behavior as they exist in real life, without distortion or embellishment. Relies on the so-called fourth wall, an imagined barrier between the audience and performers that the production always respects and maintains.

Richard the Third Malevolent title character in Shakespeare's *The Life and Death of King Richard the Third*.

Richard Schechner American director, theatre critic, and academic whose theories provided vocabulary and encouragement for immersive and site-specific performances.

Richard Wagner German opera composer and librettist whose call for artistic unity in production led to the development of the modern theatre director. Wagner was highly influential in the world of music, creating a collection of four operas called the Ring Cycle that continues to be widely performed in adventurous productions throughout the world. Unfortunately, Wagner's antisemitism taints and overshadows his artistic achievements.

Robert Wilson American director of *Einstein on the Beach* and many other works of opera and theatre known for their multidisciplinary structure, minimalist design, and precision of movement and gesture.

Samuel Beckett Irish writer whose best-known play is *Waiting for Godot*. Associated with Absurdism.

Schaubühne Major state-supported theatre in Berlin.

SITI Company Founded in 1992 by Anne Bogart and Japanese director, Tadashi Suzuki, to foster international artistic exchange and generate experimental contemporary theatre.

Sleep No More Immersive theatre production based in part on Shakespeare's *The Tragedy of Macbeth* and staged in a vacant hotel in New York.

Stanley Kowalski Chauvinistic male character in *A Streetcar Named Desire*. Famously portrayed on film by Marlon Brando.

Susanne Kennedy German director whose experimental productions explore the intersection of technology, media, and human behavior.

Table work Usually the first phase of a rehearsal process, where the director, actors, and creative team gather to read and explore a play.

The Empty Space Peter Brook's 1968 book in which he suggests theatre dispense with complex production elements and artifice in order to prioritize the actor and the spectator's engagement with him.

The Seagull Anton Chekhov's 1896 play that he insisted on calling a comedy, despite its serious overtones. Characters in the play vigorously debate the nature and purpose of art—a reflection of Chekhov's own struggle to find his dramatic voice. Yet the play is also populated with figures like Medvedenko and Masha, who seem uninterested in these squabbles and more invested in loving and being loved. Simply put, *The Seagull* is a play about art and love.

The Wooster Group Experimental theatre company, founded in 1975 in New York, that creates postmodern, self-aware productions often in conversation with classical plays. Media and technology figure prominently in the company's work.

Thomas Ostermeier German director known for bold contemporary productions of classical plays, especially a series of Shakespeare and Ibsen stagings. Artistic director of the Schaubühne theatre in Berlin.

Torvald Nora's husband in *A Doll's House*.

Trajal Harrell American choreographer and performer who rose to prominence with a series of works exploring vogueing, a dance style that emerged in Harlem as a celebration of the Black LGBTQI+ community.

Uncle Vanya Anton Chekhov's 1899 play about social isolation, personal stagnation, and feeling trapped in a cycle of life you cannot escape.